WORLD HISTORY

The Red Scare

By Andrew A. Kling

LUCENT BOOKS
A part of Gale, Cengage Learning

GALE
CENGAGE Learning·

Detroit • New York • San Francisco • New Haven, Conn • Waterville, Maine • London

LIBRARY OF CONGRESS CATALOGING-IN-PUBLICATION DATA

Kling, Andrew A., 1961-
  The red scare / by Andrew A. Kling.
    p. cm. -- (World history)
  Includes bibliographical references and index.
  ISBN 978-1-4205-0680-8 (hardcover)
  1. Anti-communist movements--United States--History--20th century--Juvenile literature.
  2. Subversive activities--United States--History--20th century--Juvenile literature.
  3. Internal security--United States--History--20th century--Juvenile literature.. I. Title.
  E743.5.K56 2011
  327.12097309'04--dc23
                                                    2011030510

Lucent Books
27500 Drake Rd.
Farmington Hills, MI 48331

ISBN-13: 978-1-4205-0680-8
ISBN-10: 1-4205-0680-3

Contents

Foreword

Each year, on the first day of school, nearly every history teacher faces the task of explaining why his or her students should study history. Many reasons have been given. One is that lessons exist in the past from which contemporary society can benefit and learn. Another is that exploration of the past allows us to see the origins of our customs, ideas, and institutions. Concepts such as democracy, ethnic conflict, or even things as trivial as fashion or mores, have historical roots.

Reasons such as these impress few students, however. If anything, these explanations seem remote and dull to young minds. Yet history is anything but dull. And therein lies what is perhaps the most compelling reason for studying history: History is filled with great stories. The classic themes of literature and drama—love and sacrifice, hatred and revenge, injustice and betrayal, adversity and overcoming adversity—fill the pages of history books, feeding the imagination as well as any of the great works of fiction do.

The story of the Children's Crusade, for example, is one of the most tragic in history. In 1212 Crusader fever hit Europe. A call went out to the pope that all good Christians should journey to Jerusalem to drive out the hated Muslims and return the city to Christian control. Heeding the call, thousands of children made the journey. Parents bravely allowed many children to go, and entire communities were inspired by the faith of these small Crusaders. Unfortunately, many boarded ships captained by slave traders, who enthusiastically sold the children into slavery as soon as they arrived at their destination. Thousands died from disease, exposure, and starvation on the long march across Europe to the Mediterranean Sea. Others perished at sea.

Another story, from a modern and more familiar place, offers a soul-wrenching view of personal humiliation but also the ability to rise above it. Hatsuye Egami was one of 110,000 Japanese Americans sent to internment camps during World War II. "Since yesterday we Japanese have ceased to be human beings," he wrote in his diary. "We are numbers. We are no longer Egamis, but the number 23324. A tag with that number is on every trunk, suitcase and bag. Tags, also, on our breasts." Despite such dehumanizing treatment, most internees worked hard to control their bitterness. They created workable communities inside the camps and demonstrated again and again their loyalty as Americans.

These are but two of the many stories from history that can be found in the pages of the Lucent Books World History series. All World History titles rely on sound research and verifiable evidence, and all give students a clear sense of time, place, and chronology through maps and time-lines as well as text.

All titles include a wide range of authoritative perspectives that demonstrate the complexity of historical interpretation and sharpen the reader's critical thinking skills. Formally documented quotations and annotated bibliographies enable students to locate and evaluate sources, often instantaneously via the Internet, and serve as valuable tools for further research and debate.

Finally, Lucent's World History titles present rousing good stories, featuring vivid primary source quotations drawn from unique, sometimes obscure sources such as diaries, public records, and contemporary chronicles. In this way, the voices of participants and witnesses as well as important biographers and historians bring the study of history to life. As we are caught up in the lives of others, we are reminded that we too are characters in the ongoing human saga, and we are better prepared for our own roles.

Important Dates at the Time of

1917
The United States enters World War I. Protests sweep cities in the Russian Empire over the war and food and energy shortages. Czar Nicholas II resigns. Bolsheviks take power.

1918
Treaty of Brest-Litovsk ends fighting between Germany and Russia. World War I ends with armistice in November. Spanish influenza pandemic kills 50 million to 100 million people worldwide (roughly 3 to 6 percent of the total population).

1932
Mohandas Gandhi begins hunger strike in India to protest British colonial treatment of lowest class of Indians. Women get the right to vote in Brazil and Uruguay.

1914
"The Great War" (today known as World War I) begins in Europe.

1927
Charles Lindbergh makes first nonstop transatlantic flight from North America to Europe.

1910

1920

1930

1915
Albert Einstein formulates his General Theory of Relativity, $E=mc^2$.

1920
First commercial radio broadcast. Women get the right to vote in United States. Final "Palmer Raids" take place across United States in effort to round up radicals and subversives. Communist Party of the USA founded in Chicago.

1924
V. I. Lenin dies; succeeded by Joseph Stalin as head of Soviet Union.

1933
Franklin D. Roosevelt inaugurated as U.S. president. Adolf Hitler elected chancellor of Germany.

the Red Scare

1939
World War II begins. "Popular Front" of communism in the United States ends following Nazi-Soviet nonaggression pact.

1950
Korean War breaks out. Senator Joseph McCarthy declares that U.S. State Dept. is harboring known Communists.

1945
Franklin Roosevelt dies and is succeeded by vice president Harry S. Truman. War ends in Europe with surrender of Germany in May. United States drops two atomic bombs on Japan in August; Japan surrenders. Soviet-style governments appear throughout Eastern Europe. Percy Spencer patents the microwave oven. Winston Churchill loses reelection as British prime minister.

1953
Tenzing Norgay and Edmund Hillary are first to climb to the top of Mt. Everest.

1954
Army-McCarthy hearings take place in U.S. Senate. Algerian war for independence from France begins. French colonial forces leave Vietnam.

1940   **1950**   **1960**

1935
Italy invades Ethiopia.

1946
Churchill makes "Iron Curtain" speech in Fulton, MO.

1949
Chinese Communists defeat Chinese Nationalists; establish Communist government in China. Soviet Union tests atomic bomb.

1957
Joseph R. McCarthy dies in Washington, D.C.

1947
U.S. House Committee on Un-American Activities finds the "Hollywood Ten" in contempt of Congress. British colonial era ends in South Asia with independence of India and Pakistan.

1955
Dr. Jonas Salk announces development of vaccine for polio. Disneyland opens in California. "Rock Around the Clock" becomes first rock-and-roll song to top U.S. music charts.

Introduction

Milo Radulovich

Milo Radulovich was like many Americans in the 1950s. He was the son of immigrants; his father was an auto worker who had come to America from Serbia. Milo grew up in the 1930s and attended Michigan State College as an aviation cadet before joining the U.S. Army's Air Corps in 1944, when World War II was in its fifth year. Radulovich became a meteorologist for the Air Corps and remained in the armed forces until 1952, performing top-secret work before he was discharged as a first lieutenant.

After serving his country, he returned to his hometown, got married, had a family, and worked to continue his education, this time at the University of Michigan. He also joined the United States Air Force Reserve. In August 1953, an air force major came to the door of his home in Dexter, Michigan. The officer handed Radulovich a letter that said that he was being expelled from the air force reserve because he was a security risk. This decision was based not on anything he had done but on who he knew. The air force was discharging him because he refused to cut ties with his father and his sister.

Both his father and sister were Americans, but the air force contended that their activities were suspicious and possibly dangerous to national security. Radulovich's Serbian-born father read a Serbian-language newspaper that recounted news of his homeland; he also liked the calendar that came with the subscription. His sister was involved in civil rights causes and had been photographed picketing a Detroit hotel for its refusal to lodge the black singer and social activist Paul Robeson, who some observers considered anti-American for his advocacy of equal rights for all Americans as well as for his political views. His father's and sister's activities led the U.S. government to contend that Radulovich's relationship with them meant that he posed a security risk to the nation.

Radulovich was not alone. At that time, thousands of individuals from all walks of life were the subjects of investigations and allegations about their past and present lives. Citizens scrutinized their elected officials, friends, neighbors, and family members for such suspected subversive activities as belonging to a group that advocated equal rights for African Americans and other minorities, participating in an association that worked for better international relations, or participating in labor union activities that sought better wages or working conditions. Newspapers and magazines that specialized in international relations or that were published in foreign languages were suspected of spreading subversive anti-American agendas. Some critics also accused such well-respected daily newspapers as the *Washington Post* and the *New York Times* of being anti-American because of their dedication to objective and unbiased reporting. It was all part of the international reaction to communism; a reaction historians have labeled "The Red Scare."

Radulovich was not investigated for what he read or what he did but because of who he knew. Radulovich denied that he was a security risk or a Communist and fought the accusations. His story was picked up by the *Detroit News* and shortly thereafter came to the attention of pioneering television newsman Edward R. Murrow. Murrow had been searching for a story that exemplified how the Red Scare was affecting average Americans, and he used Radulovich's story in an episode of his *See It Now* news program.

The broadcast pointed out that Radulovich was not a Communist and that the air force was not accusing him of being one. It showed that the government determined that he was a risk simply because of what others close to him had done. This practice of guilt by association was typical of the Red Scare period. Suspicion, fear, paranoia, and conspiracy theories abounded as people from all walks of life reacted to the existence and growth of communism. By the 1950s, communism as a political and economic philosophy was a way of life in the Soviet Union, and it was spreading to other countries around the world. Indeed, many Americans believed that, unless something was done and vigorous measures were taken, democracy in the United States could be replaced by communism.

Chapter One

The Rise of the "Reds"

The year 1917 was an eventful one. The zipper was invented and patented by a Swedish scientist. In the United States, Marshmallow Fluff and Lincoln Logs hit store shelves. The forklift and the electric drill were invented. Babe Ruth, pitching for baseball's Boston Red Sox, won twenty-four games. In Canada, a group of businessmen and athletes formed the National Hockey League. In Europe, the United States joined the Allies to fight Germany and the Central Powers during the "Great War" (now called World War I), which had been raging since 1914. And in the Russian Empire, a revolution was brewing that would shape world history for nearly a century and that would lead to the periods called the Red Scare.

The Fall of Imperial Russia

The Russian Empire had been ruled for centuries by monarchs called "czars." In early 1917, Russia's involvement in the Great War was not going well. Czar Nicholas II was beset by defeats on the battlefield and political unrest at home. The Russians' successes early in the war were followed by German counterattacks, and inadequate supplies led to staggering losses. Morale plummeted among the Russian troops. The czar's secret police reported in October 1916 that "everybody is waiting impatiently for the end to this [war]. . . . There is a marked increase in hostile feelings among the [troops], not only against the government, but against all other social groups."[1]

By 1917, Russia had suffered almost 6 million casualties from the war. Thousands of deserters streamed into cities such as Moscow and Petrograd, the imperial capital (formerly, and again today, St. Petersburg), hoping to escape the horrors of war. Instead, they found that conditions at home were no better. Disease and hunger were rampant, along

The reign of Csar Nicholas II was ended in 1917 by war-weary citizens who opposed the Russian monarchy.

with severe food and energy shortages. The czar's government seemed unable to solve the problems, which led to mass protests. In February 1917, nearly 250,000 protesters in Petrograd were joined by the local army units, leaving only two thousand police to defend the city. The protesters, now equipped with armored cars and machine guns, convened the "Soviet (or "Council") of Workers' and Soldiers' Deputies" to determine what their demands were and what their next move should be.

Czar Nicholas II resigned in March, appointing a temporary government to run the country and to continue the war effort. The new government, however, could not feed the citizens or reform the ancient political system. The calls for change continued to grow. One of the loudest calls came from a group called the Bolsheviks. They were led by the charismatic Vladimir I. Ulyanov, who went by the nickname of "Lenin." He declared that Russia's only alternative to the imperial government was one based on socialism.

Socialism and Communism

Socialism was not a new concept in 1917. It had been born in the social, political, and economic upheavals of the nineteenth century. At that time, employees had few laws protecting their rights. Workers were not guaranteed a minimum wage and pay rates were subject to the whims of employers. For example, in 1893 and 1894, the Pullman Company, which built railroad cars, cut employees' pay between 25 and 33 percent, while continuing to pay dividends to its investors. Workers were often expected to work up to twelve hours a day, six days a week, with only Sundays free. Overtime pay was an almost unheard-of concept. Historian Barbara W. Tuchman described one woman's employment in 1887 as "sewing in a factory ten and a half hours a day for $2.50 a week,"[2] which equaled forty-two cents a day, or four cents an hour (equivalent to about ninety-nine cents an hour in 2011). Joining a union, or even talking about creating a union, could lead to being fired on the spot.

Capitalism drove the economies of industrialized nations such as the United States and Great Britain, but it was subject to boom and bust cycles. It often left a few people with great wealth and the vast majority with much less. Social scientists and philosophers around the world who studied economics, such as Friedrich Engels and Karl Marx, theorized that just as capitalism had replaced earlier economic systems, capitalism eventually must be replaced by one that was more equitable to workers.

Marx and Engels believed that this new system would reverse the control of the economy. Under capitalism, the bourgeoisie (pronounced "boor-zwa-ZEE") owned the world's resources, such as factories, mills, mines, and farms; in the new economy, the resources would be in the hands of the proletariat, who were the millions of workers around the world. They called this idea *socialism* and believed it would eventually lead to a society without nations or economic classes, called *communism*. Politically, socialism was part of the left wing, or liberal, political spectrum; most capitalists and industrialists were at the other end, the conservative right wing.

By 1917 many workers in heavily industrialized nations were attracted to socialism. It promised that they would be able to control their own pay and working conditions instead of being dependent on their current employers. For nearly thirty years before the Great War, strikes and Socialist rallies had blossomed in cities such as Chicago, London, and Paris. Leftist participants marched by the thousands, carrying red banners, the chosen color of socialism and workers' rights.

V. I. Lenin

Vladimir Ilyich Ulyanov, better known as "Lenin," was a lawyer, author, and economic theorist before becoming the leader of the Bolshevik Revolution and the founder of the Soviet Union. Born in Simbirsk, Russia, in 1870, his well-educated, middle-class parents instructed him and his siblings about human rights and the struggle for a free society. He became an antigovernment radical following his brother's execution in 1887 in connection with a plot to assassinate the czar.

He received a law degree in 1892 and read the works of Karl Marx, Friedrich Engels, and other revolutionary writers. The following year, he moved to the Russian capital of St. Petersburg, where he practiced law and worked with other Marxists. He was arrested in 1895 for plotting against the czar and was imprisoned and exiled to Siberia until 1900, where he wrote extensively about Marxism and revolutionary politics. He lived in several European cities from 1900 to 1905; he took the pseudonym Lenin in 1902, from the Lena River in Siberia, the year his landmark work *What Is to Be Done?* was published.

Lenin returned to Russia after the fall of the czar in 1917. He led the nation until his death from complications of a stroke in 1924.

A New Convert to Socialism

Pete Muselin became a Socialist after the Great War. His family had immigrated to the United States from Croatia in eastern Europe and had settled in a steel-milling town in Pennsylvania in 1912. In 1917, he joined the U.S. Army and spent almost two years in France. He recalled that

> the war and everything about it overwhelmed me. I began to ask myself very seriously: What am I doing in France? After all, I don't know a single person in the enemy lines. They haven't harmed me in any way whatsoever. . . . What could be the reason we were killing each other? I couldn't conceive of anything more stupid than a war, human beings killing other human beings without any apparent reason. But the more I thought about it, the more I understood the underlying cause: War is predicated on profit. After I got back in 1919, I saw the fallacy of this war ending all wars and making the world safe for democracy. To me, it was clear that all these slogans were false. I became involved in the socialist movement.

Pete Muselin. "The Steel Fist in a Pennsylvania Company Town." In Bud Schultz and Ruth Schultz. *It Did Happen Here: Recollections of Political Repression in America.* Berkeley and Los Angeles: University of California Press, 1989, pp. 68–69.

Reds

As Socialist protests grew, politicians and industry leaders became concerned. They began to call the protesters "Reds." They usually meant it as an insult, because the protesters were seen as a threat to business and society. Factory owners accused them of making unreasonable demands for higher wages, and law enforcement officials accused them of stirring up discontent.

The term *Reds* caught on with newspapers and magazines around the world.

Soon, however, the protesters started calling themselves "Reds" as well. The term was a badge of honor, reflecting commitment to their cause. Supporters of socialism spread their philosophies through books, pamphlets, and newspapers; in the days before electronic communications, the printed word was the most effective means of sharing information. Their publications proclaimed that their protests and strikes against the bourgeoisie were a means of accelerating the inevitable coming of socialism and the eventual development of the Communist state of total equality.

Lenin and his fellow Bolsheviks were also Reds. They proudly proclaimed their support for Russia's working men and women. They believed that the only way Russia could survive and move forward in the modern world was with a Socialist government directed by the proletariat.

The Bolshevik Revolution

After Nicholas's abdication, the Bolsheviks' popularity grew in the cities and in the countryside. Their pledge to end Russian involvement in the war was particularly popular among war-weary soldiers and factory workers. They promised that the country's huge estates, owned by the rich but farmed by the poor, would be divided equally among those who worked the land—an idea that was popular among rural populations. By creating and manipulating a nationwide network of workers' and soldiers' soviets, the Bolsheviks extended their influence across the former empire.

In November 1917, they overthrew the provisional government to take control of the entire Russian state. More Russians joined the Bolsheviks after the latter negotiated the Treaty of Brest-Litovsk

Lenin addresses a crowd in Moscow's Red Square in October 1917. By the next month, the Bolsheviks had overthrown Russia's provisional government to take control of the nation, sparking a civil war.

Who Were the Bolsheviks?

The word *bolshevik* derives from the Russian word *bolshinstvo*, meaning "majority." The word was applied to one of the two factions of the Russian Social Democratic Labor Party before and during World War I. At a party conference in London and Brussels in 1903, a group led by V.I. Lenin advocated that membership in the party should be limited to a small group of professional revolutionaries who would spend their time organizing a mass uprising against the czarist government. The opposition advocated party membership to anyone who wanted to support the cause, and it generally favored working with other political groups, which Lenin opposed.

The party split into two factions; the majority of conference attendees became known as the Bolsheviks; the minority became the Mensheviks (from the Russian for "minority"). At first, the split was amicable, and the Bolsheviks held a small majority during party meetings, but after 1905, the rift became permanent, and the two held separate party conferences thereafter. The Bolsheviks gained increasing popular support during the 1910s among Socialists and factory workers and by 1917 was the leading voice among Russia's Socialist parties.

with Germany in March 1918, which removed Russia from the fighting.

The Bolsheviks soon discovered that ruling Russia was not an easy task, however. Many Russians were not interested in a Socialist or Communist society. Others were members of ethnic minority groups who wanted independence from Russian rule. Soon, Russia was embroiled in a civil war.

Red Against White

The Russian Civil War pitted the Red Bolsheviks against the "White Russians." Some Whites were right-wing conservatives who advocated a return to the czarist system of government; others were in favor of a more moderate, left-leaning, Western-style democracy. But all were opposed to Lenin's Bolsheviks. The Whites took their rallying color from the first czar, Ivan III (1462–1505), who was known as "The White King."

Throughout the winter of 1917–1918, the Bolsheviks' militia, called the Red Guards, fought skirmishes with the Whites' Volunteer Army in western and southern Russia and Ukraine. The Whites were led by several former Imperial Army generals who had escaped from Bolshevik prisons, but they were hampered by shortages in personnel and equipment. The Red Guard units were led by Great War veterans who had first-hand experience with modern equipment. According to historian W. Bruce

Red Guards supporting the Bolshevik government patrol Petrograd in their civil war against "White Russians," who preferred either a return of the monarchy or a move towards democracy.

Lincoln, when the Red offensive began on Christmas Day 1917, its assault group "numbered more than twenty thousand," outnumbering the Whites by more than two to one, and was supported "by more than a hundred machine guns, nearly twenty field guns [artillery], five airplanes, and an armored train."[3]

Red Guard victories over the White Volunteer Army continued throughout the winter of 1917–1918. By the spring, Lenin felt confident to report, "It can be said with certainty that, in the main, the civil war has ended." Some new skirmishes might break out, he said, "but there is no doubt that on the internal front reaction has been irretrievably smashed by the efforts of the insurgent people."[4] His optimism was short-lived, however, as the new Socialist regime of Soviet Russia soon faced new challenges.

International Opposition

These new challenges came from both former enemies and allies in the Great War. Lenin believed that a Russian treaty with Germany would lead to peace in Western Europe, where Germany was fighting the czar's former allies—Great Britain, France, and the United States. The end of the war, he felt, would lead to more Socialist revolutions. In a speech to the Soviet of Workers' and Soldiers' Deputies in the city of Petrograd, Lenin hailed the growing workers' movement that was "already beginning to develop in Italy, England, and Germany," and concluded with, "Long live the worldwide socialist revolution!"[5]

Lenin knew that achieving a worldwide revolution would be difficult and warned that Bolshevik rule would not go unchallenged internationally. Indeed, during the negotiations over the Treaty of Brest-Litovsk, German troops overran and occupied large areas of western and southern Russia. But Germany was only part of the problem. According to historian Evan Mawdsley, following the revolution, "Allied-Soviet relations were never good. The Bolsheviks hated the Allies; for them [the Allies] meant imperialism. The Western statesmen despised what the revolution stood for, and, more important, were outraged by Russia's betrayal of the wartime alliance."[6]

The Allied leaders believed that they had little reason to trust the new regime in Russia. They felt betrayed by the Treaty of Brest-Litovsk. The end of fighting with Russia meant Germany would redirect resources to Western Europe at a time when the outcome of the war remained in doubt.

Additionally, newspaper stories and refugee accounts spread news and rumors about life under the Reds. The Bolsheviks seemed to be just as ruthless as the czarist government. Eyewitnesses spoke of mass arrests and assassinations, as well as the rumor that Bolshevik supporters had imprisoned and executed the czar and his family, all in the name of the Socialist revolution. Consequently, the Allies began to see an evolving struggle between the Bolsheviks' socialism and Western capitalism.

"Our Real Danger Now Is ... Bolshevism"

The Allied leaders were ardent supporters of the capitalist system. Some, like U.S. president Woodrow Wilson, were left-leaning concerning human rights; others, like British prime minister David Lloyd George, were more conservative. But all of the leaders had financial and political support from industrialists or were businessmen themselves. So they were opposed to the Bolsheviks' far left Socialist and Communist ideals. Additionally, they feared that the success of the Bolsheviks in Russia might encourage Reds in other countries to try a similar revolution.

Historian Stephen M. Walt sums up the opinions of the Allied leaders:

According to [British] General Sir Henry Wilson, chief of the Imperial General staff, by October 1918 the British Cabinet was united in the belief that "our real danger now is not the [Germans] but Bolshevism." Other Allied officials held similar views. Woodrow Wilson told his Cabinet that "the spirit of the Bolshevik[s] is lurking everywhere." U.S. secretary of state Robert Lansing described Bolshevism as "the most hideous and monstrous thing that the human mind has ever conceived" and lamented that it was now "spreading westward." The commander of the Allied armies, [French] Marshal Ferdinand Foch, warned against "the horrors of Bolshevism.". . . Lloyd George reportedly believed that revolution in England was not out of the question ... and Wilson regarded Central Europe as especially vulnerable.[7]

An anti-Communist political cartoon from 1918 depicts a wounded Russian bear on a stretcher being carried by the Allies. Troops from the United States, Britain, and France joined White Russian forces in their failed attempt to defeat the Bolshevik movement.

All of these opinions led the Allied leaders to intervene in Russian affairs. They believed that the Red revolution needed to be stopped and the Bolsheviks removed from power.

Allied Intervention

The Allies began their campaign to end the Bolshevik revolution before the end of 1917 by providing the Whites with financial and equipment assistance. By August 1918, British, French, and American forces had landed at the ports of Murmansk, Arkhangelsk, and Vladivostok, and Allied troops had joined White forces in southern Russia.

The Allied effort was hampered from the start, however, by poor organization, lack of synchronization among member nations, and war-weary troops. The Whites soon discovered that the French brigades sent to help them were in no mood to fight on foreign soil. The British were plagued by the language barrier as they tried to train White Russians to fight the Bolsheviks. One British officer said sarcastically, "It was truly a stroke of genius for our War Office to flood us with officers and men as instructors for the new Russian army, scarcely one of whom could speak a word of Russian."[8]

After Germany surrendered in November 1918, ending the Great War, Allied troops remained in Russia. Far from their homes, and far from the public eye, they fought piece-meal actions against the Bolsheviks, without coordinated actions or clear objectives. Soon, Allied leaders realized that such a campaign was not only expensive but politically unpopular at home. The White Russians had failed to overthrow the Reds and, even with Allied support, were unable to threaten Soviet expansion into the south and east of Russia.

The last of the Allied troops left Russia in 1920. But the withdrawal did not mean that opposition to the Bolsheviks' Socialist revolution ended. Instead, anti-Red campaigns took on a different form, and soon events much closer to home became front-page news.

Reds in the News

Americans in the early twentieth century received their news primarily from newspapers. There were over twenty-two thousand newspapers in the United States in 1918. Large cities such as New York and Chicago had several competing daily newspapers. Many newspapers put out several editions throughout the day and into the evening to cover breaking stories and rushed out special editions, called "extras," with the latest developments. Bold headlines in huge letters dominated the front pages to catch readers' eyes.

During the war, sensational headlines had screamed about German atrocities; warned of German spies, plots, and sabotage; and highlighted American bravery and patriotism. But as 1918 passed into 1919, increasing numbers of headlines included "Reds" or "Bolsheviks" and the threat of left-wing socialism, dubbed the "Red Menace."

Sometimes the headlines spoke of political unrest overseas. They declared that "Bolshevism Is Spreading"[9] as German leftists, hoping to play a role in the postwar government, tried to set up local governments along Soviet lines. One Socialist group, led by a German who adopted the pen name "Spartacus" (the name of a slave who led a revolt in ancient Rome), called themselves "Spartacides" or "Spartacists." But in January 1919 when *The New York Times* reported armed conflicts erupting in cities such as Munich and Berlin, there was also a small item noting that the local Spartacides had adopted a new nickname: "Communists."

Reds were also making headlines in the United States. Socialists had been active in unions for decades. Many politicians and industrialists believed that unions were hotbeds of Red activity. In early 1919, when union workers struck for higher wages from Lawrence, Massachusetts to San Francisco, California, they believed that Reds were the instigators. In Seattle, Washington, a general strike in February shut down the city, as more than sixty thousand workers from over a hundred unions left their jobs for four days. Seattle mayor Ole Hanson declared that the strike was "an attempt at the overthrow of Government and [was] the foundation of Bolshevism and Russian Soviet rule,"[10] and

Steel workers demonstrate during their strike in Pittsburgh, Pennsylvania, in 1919, one of several strikes by unions across the United States that year. Some politicians and industrialists cited the influence of socialists among unions as part of a "Red Menace" that threatened the nation.

when it ended peacefully, he proclaimed that Americanism had won over Bolshevism. All this agitation by workers did not go unnoticed by U.S. government officials, either, and the government's response grabbed even more headlines.

"To Incite the Overthrow of the Government"

In early 1919, a U.S. Senate committee designed to "inquire into any effort to incite the overthrow of the Government of this country"[11] heard from over two dozen witnesses who shared their views of the suspected Red Menace. The witnesses' stories led to headlines blaring the "Horrors of Bolshevism,"[12] "Mass Terror by Bolshevik[s],"[13] and that "Riffraff Rules in Russia."[14] The committee's final report, released in June 1919, was more than twelve hundred pages long. But the report did very little to expose efforts in America to usurp democracy. According to historian Robert K. Murray, "The report represented merely another sensational exposé of Russian bolshevism

J. Edgar Hoover

Washington, D.C., native J. Edgar Hoover began his career with the federal government in 1913 with the Library of Congress before moving to the Justice Department in 1917. There he showed an amazing aptitude for compiling and indexing information, which brought him to the attention of attorney general A. Mitchell Palmer. Working for Palmer, Hoover compiled a card file of over four hundred thousand suspected radicals and assembled an impressive network of informants across the country.

Following the so-called Palmer Raids on Communist organizations and people, Hoover continued to compile information about Socialists as well as the newly formed Communist Party of the USA. In a briefing paper, Hoover expressed his personal opinions about the goals and activities of the new party, writing:

> These [Communist] doctrines threaten the happiness of the community, the safety of every individual, and the continuance of every home and fireside. They would destroy the peace of the country and thrust it into a condition of anarchy and lawlessness and immorality that passes imagination.

In 1924, Hoover was appointed as the director of the Bureau of Investigation, which was renamed the Federal Bureau of Investigation (FBI) in 1935.

Quoted in William A. Klingaman. *Encyclopedia of the McCarthy Era.*(New York: Facts On File, 1996, p. 181.

and a complete denunciation of that system."[15]

One of the hearings' participants was President Wilson's attorney general, A. Mitchell Palmer. His actions drew headlines over the next several months. For example, in August, Palmer created the General Intelligence Division within the Justice Department's Bureau of Investigation (the predecessor of today's FBI) and charged it with investigating the programs of radical groups and identifying their members.

Palmer picked a twenty-four-year-old Justice Department employee named J. Edgar Hoover to head the new division. Hoover had spent the war investigating suspected enemy agents, and this new assignment suited his skills perfectly. He studied arrest records, union membership rolls, political affiliations, and subscription lists of publications deemed to be radical in nature. He hired translators to read American foreign-language newspapers. He also recruited and employed undercover informants and used illegal wiretaps to gather information.

The result was a list of hundreds of thousands of suspected Reds and other radicals that Hoover and Palmer felt should be rounded up, arrested, prosecuted, and expelled from the United States. Palmer chose November 7, 1919, for the first wave of raids, because it was the second anniversary of the Bolshevik Revolution.

The "Palmer Raids"

From November 1919 to January 1920, federal agents, assisted by local police, struck their targets in what are now called the "Palmer Raids." According to author and journalist Ann Hagedorn,

> On January 2, in thirty-three cities, in twenty-three states, in clubhouses, poolhalls, restaurants, bowling alleys, and even bedrooms, as many as six thousand aliens, suspected to be dangerous radicals, were swept into Palmer's net of security. . . . Palmer's raiders herded them into detention centers, separating families, sometimes inflicting severe injuries, and holding them for days without access to counsel.[16]

One of those arrested on January 2 in Philadelphia was a Lithuanian immigrant named Sonia Kaross. She worked as a bookkeeper for a Lithuanian-language Socialist newspaper, and her husband worked for a railroad. Both were members of the Socialist Party and participated in party-sponsored community activities. They and their friends read about the earlier raids and wondered if it could happen to them. When it did, it caught them by surprise.

> [At] one o'clock [in the morning], there was banging on the doors. It woke up the whole building. There were police cars and all kinds of detectives all over the street. They came in and took all my books, all my letters, whatever they found. They took everything, every little paper they could get hold of. They threw it all into big bags. . . . They

just threw everything in there and took them away, and I could never get anything back.

Then they took me and my husband away. I was almost seven months pregnant.[17]

It is important to remember that it was not illegal to be a member of the Socialist Party; nor was it illegal to be a member of the Communist Party of America (later called the Communist Party of the USA, or CPUSA), which had been formed the previous September. Palmer, Hoover, and others opposed to leftists, however, believed that the members and supporters of these parties were the heart of the Red Menace and were actively advocating the overthrow of the U.S. government. They believed these groups needed to be eliminated. But the January 2 event was the last Palmer Raid, and the Red Menace seemed to fade from view.

The Legacy of the Palmer Raids

Today, historians see the Palmer Raids as the end of the postwar Red Scare (sometimes called the first Red Scare). The January 2 roundup was the last raid, because as 1920 progressed, leftist agitation decreased nationwide. A postwar economic boom began, and unions called for fewer strikes as wages rose and inflation stabilized. The Red Menace left the front pages.

The raids had been touted in nationwide headlines, but they also drew criticism for their heavy-handed tactics. Government attorneys and law professionals denounced the raids, believing that they had trampled on the civil rights of those detained. As Hagedorn notes, "A large percentage of the men and women taken that day had nothing to do with Bolshevism,"[18] and just happened to be in the wrong place at the wrong time. Sonia Kaross's story is typical: she and her husband were in jail for nearly three months during the legal wrangling, and she miscarried during her arrest. Eventually their cases were thrown out and they were released.

The Palmer Raids created a lasting legacy, however. The raids and the press coverage reinforced the perception that existed throughout the Red Scare period that Communists, Socialists, and other radicals were, indeed, everywhere. Additionally, they forced leftists to keep a low profile in the years to come due to the development of "Red Squads." These were special teams of officers in law enforcement organizations, particularly police departments in large cities such as New York and Chicago, whose sole task was to monitor the activities of Communist and Socialist groups in their jurisdictions. Red Squads were often supported or financed by anti-Red business leaders, who continued to believe that Reds were ubiquitous and a threat to the nation.

The Red Squads shared their information with the Bureau of Investigation, which continued to gather information on suspected individuals and groups. The Bureau and Red Squads routinely raided suspected meetings of CPUSA and arrested radicals throughout the 1920s. Efforts by Red Squads and other anti-Communist groups led the CPUSA to diligently keep its membership secret and its members safe from arrest, while continuing to keep in contact with the Russian Communist Party for direction and for funding. Events at the end of the 1920s and throughout the 1930s, however, enabled the CPUSA to play a greater role in American society than ever before.

The Great Depression

The 1930s proved to be the high point for the Communist Party in the USA. After the stock market crash of 1929 and the worldwide depression that followed, businesses failed by the thousands, throwing millions out of work. The capitalist system was at its lowest point, and it seemed that nothing could be done to end the downturn.

The Great Depression stretched on into the 1930s; while programs of President Franklin D. Roosevelt's New Deal helped, millions of workers still struggled to survive. The CPUSA gained new members among those who felt that capitalism had failed them. As historian Ellen Schrecker put it, "There was, it was alleged, no unemployment in the Soviet Union and it seemed possible that

A man carries a sign urging Americans to join the Communist Party of the USA (CPUSA) at a demonstration in the 1930s. The Great Depression prompted many people to join the CPUSA, as they blamed the nation's economic woes on failed capitalist policies.

communism might well offer a solution to the devastation the Depression had wrought."[19] Additionally, as the New Deal began to put people back to work, the U.S. government began working in partnership with labor unions. Because of the CPUSA's strong background in labor organizing, it gathered even more members from union workers. The party worked to unionize dock workers in San Francisco, steelworkers in Birmingham, AL, and autoworkers in Detroit. Many of the unions joined the Congress of Industrial Organizations (CIO), which was a newer alternative to the decades-old American Federation of Labor (AFL).

These successes did not go unnoticed, however. The efforts of Communists were met with opposition through a process called "red-baiting."

Red-Baiting

Red-baiting, the practice of accusing an individual or group of being Communist, rose to new heights during the Depression. Although being a Communist or a member of the CPUSA was not illegal, it was very unpopular because such activity was seen as anti-democratic and anti-American. Red-baiters often targeted labor leaders, civil rights advocates, and liberal educators. Some

"Communists"

In the volatile political world that followed World War I, Socialist groups split apart over issues of doctrine and interpretation. In Germany, a group of Socialists decided to adopt the label "Communist"; soon the new name was being adopted by Socialists around the world inspired by the Russian Revolution. For example, the *New York Times* ran an article on September 4, 1919, which described the formation of the "Communist Labor Party of America" at a convention in Chicago. During the debate over a name for the new group, one of the delegates, H. Tichenor, said, "There are fifty-seven varieties of socialism, and perhaps more than that, but there is only one kind of Bolshevism, and the world is having a hard time to stomach that. Communism knows no race, nation, breed, or creed. We've got to get the word 'communism' in the name some place."

This group eventually merged with other Socialist factions by 1925 to form the Communist Party of the USA. The adoption of the word *Communist* soon meant that reporters, editors, and Americans at large began to equate that name with the epithets "Red" and "Bolshevik" already in use.

Quoted in New York Times. "New Party Raises Bolshevist Banner," September 4, 1919.

red-baiters were members of law enforcement, who worked in cooperation with individuals or groups attacking suspected Communists.

Individual red-baiters such as publishing magnate William Randolph Hearst, extolled the virtues of Americanism through speeches and publications. They created lists of suspected individuals and organizations and shared this data through publications and personal correspondence. For example, landing on such a list meant a business owner could lose customers, employees, or the necessary government permits to stay in business. Red-baiters also pressured state and local politicians to investigate suspected Communist influences in schools and universities. Educators who taught modern European history were often targeted, especially if they attempted to examine the rise of socialism or the Russian Revolution. Nationwide, educators finding themselves on a red-baiting list lost book contracts, speaking engagements, or, in extreme cases, their jobs. For example, in Georgia, teachers could be fired for violating a 1935 state law that prohibited the teaching of "any theory of government, of economics, or of social relations which is inconsistent with the fundamental principles of patriotism and high ideals of Americanism."[20]

Conspicuous red-baiting groups included the AFL, the American Legion, and the Catholic Church. According to Schrecker, the Legion "had been organized right after World War I specifically to crack down on radicalism."[21] Now, the group redoubled their efforts to denounce communism. Throughout the 1930s, strikes and unemployment protests were often met with physical violence by strikebreakers, who were sometimes organized by local American Legion posts. Members of the Catholic Church became red-baiters because communism championed atheism. Many church leaders were appalled by the Soviet Union's crackdown on organized religion in the 1920s and believed the United States could be headed for a similar fate. One response was to work within the labor movement. The Catholic Church established centers where Catholic workers were groomed for union leadership. Using Catholic teachings and public-speaking techniques, graduates publicized union organizers suspected of Communist leanings.

While union organizing was the CPUSA's most visible activity, red-baiters also paid attention to the party's other activities. In the 1930s, the party began to attract Americans from throughout the political spectrum through their work in "front groups."

Cadres and Front Groups

During the Depression, the CPUSA became the most organized group on the American left. It developed core groups of members, called "cadres." The cadres were sent to special training schools and either worked full-time as political organizers inside the party, within the labor unions, or in "front groups." Front groups were party-sponsored and party-run community-based activities across the United States. According to Schrecker, during the 1930s, the CPUSA was at the organizational center of a whole constellation of causes [and] organizations that ranged from the labor movement to literary magazines, to organized benevolent societies [such as] the International Workers Order that sold insurance and cemetery plots to left-wingers. There were communist summer camps, there were communist baseball teams, there were communist literary magazines, [and] there were communist dance groups.[22]

The wide range of social, political, and economic organizations that served as front groups connected the CPUSA to more Americans than ever before. For example, many American liberals who were working for social justice among minorities joined the party because of the promises of equality under communism. New members included students, teachers, professors, and entertainers. And American conservatives joined because of events abroad.

A woman reads the Sunday Worker *at the CPUSA headquarters in New York City in 1937. During the 1930s, members of the CPUSA formed cadres from which they ran community-based activities and organizations known as "front groups."*

The Popular Front

The CPUSA attracted conservatives from the American right following the rise of Adolf Hitler in Germany in 1933. The Soviet Communist Party declared that Hitler's far-right fascism was a threat to the Soviet Union and the working class, and in 1935, it adopted a program called "the Popular Front." The program's intent was to create an antifascist coalition from both the right and the left. Some conservatives, particularly a large number of American Jews, saw the CPUSA as the only group actively working against fascism. From 1936 to 1938, the party more than doubled its membership, from roughly forty thousand to eighty-two thousand.

The Popular Front and the CPUSA took a stunning blow in 1939 when the Soviet Union and Hitler's Germany signed a nonaggression pact. Suddenly, the message from Moscow was that the struggle between fascism and democracy was an imperialist struggle in which Communists need not take sides. Many who joined the party precisely because of its antifascist work now decided to leave; many liberals did as well when the Soviets began to denounce President Roosevelt's support of Great Britain when the outbreak of World War II in 1939.

But the Popular Front had a revival in 1941. Hitler invaded the Soviet Union; suddenly, Communists were antifascist again. When Japan attacked Pearl Harbor, bringing the United States into the war, Americans and Soviets became allies. Schrecker notes, "By January, 1943, one-fifth of the men in the [CPUSA] were serving in the military. Local party units were running blood drives, collecting tin cans, and selling war bonds. . . . Patriotism became the order of the day."[23]

Too Patriotic

This patriotism did not go unnoticed. In April 1945, American Communists were stunned by an article by the prominent French Communist Jacques Duclos in the French magazine *Cahiers du Communisme*. It accused American Communists of having been too American during the war; the patriotic Americanism had been too fervent, and must now stop. Although written by Duclos, the message apparently was coming directly from Moscow. The camaraderie of the Popular Front was over.

It was also apparent that the United States and the Soviet Union were now the two most powerful nations on earth. The nations' alliance frayed, crumbled, and disintegrated entirely in the succeeding years. And Americans of all political views soon discovered that a second Red Scare was taking shape.

Chapter Two

"Our Job ... Shall Be to Rout Them Out"

The Red Scare made few headlines during World War II. Red-baiters and Red hunters discovered that Americans were more interested in defeating the Allies' enemies overseas than in ferreting out Communists at home. Although the United States and the Soviet Union were allies in the war, many anti-Communists remained alert for anything that they believed might present the Soviet Union too favorably, such as in books, radio programs, news reports, or Hollywood movies. They feared that the wartime alliance had led some in America to be subverted by communism and by Soviet representatives. They wondered if the Communists had recruited American citizens or government officials to their cause. Such efforts, they believed, could lead to the expansion of communism worldwide and, perhaps, to the overthrow of American democracy.

Anti-Communists also paid close attention to the numerous wartime strategy meetings. In these conferences, the leaders of the Allies, including U.S. president Franklin D. Roosevelt (and his successor, Harry S. Truman), British prime minister Winston Churchill, and Soviet premier Joseph Stalin, agreed that the Soviets would have the task of capturing the German capital of Berlin. Consequently, in the spring of 1945, Soviet forces drove German armies out of occupied territories in Eastern Europe on their way to Berlin.

The leaders also reached a number of important agreements about what to do after the war. They decided that once Germany surrendered, the country, and Berlin itself would both be divided into four zones of occupation by the United States, Britain, France, and the Soviet Union. Additionally, they agreed that prewar nations liberated from Nazi occupation would be able to choose their new governments in free elections; however, it soon became apparent that the areas of Europe that had been liberated by Soviet troops in 1945 were heading in a direction unanticipated by Western leaders.

"From Stettin in the Baltic to Trieste in the Adriatic"

As the war ended, Soviet-style governments appeared in the nations that the Russian troops had liberated. Communists in the prewar nations of Estonia, Latvia, Lithuania, Poland, Czechoslovakia, Romania, Yugoslavia, Bulgaria, and Albania were aided by the Soviet military and the Communist Party to take the reins of power. The Soviet secret police worked with local Communists to ensure that election results would be in their favor and that any opposition movements were crushed through arrests and executions.

Stalin's rationale for these operations was both political and emotional. Russia had suffered more than 20 million casualties during World War II, and he was unwilling to subject his nation to another such catastrophe. Stalin also feared an expansion of Western-style democracy in Europe. Consequently, his postwar maneuverings led to a buffer zone of nations friendly to the Soviet Union. Stalin and his allies called it the "Eastern Bloc"; Western politicians referred to it as the "Soviet Bloc" or the "Communist Bloc."

Many in the West were alarmed by this expansion of Communist influence. In March 1946 Winston Churchill, no longer prime minister, made an historic speech at Westminster College in Fulton, Missouri. In outlining his view for a postwar world, he decried what was happening in Europe.

From Stettin [today's Szczecin, Poland,] in the Baltic to Trieste [Italy] in the Adriatic, an iron curtain has descended across the Continent. Behind that line lie all the capitals of the ancient states of Central and Eastern Europe. Warsaw, Berlin, Prague, Vienna, Budapest, Belgrade, Bucharest and Sofia, all these famous cities and the populations

A man looks at a display of Communist literature under the Soviet symbol in Prague, Czechoslovakia, in 1947. The Soviet Union drove the rise of Communist governments in that nation and others to form the Eastern Bloc in the years following World War II.

around them lie in what I must call the Soviet sphere, and all are subject in one form or another, not only to Soviet influence but to a very high and, in many cases, increasing measure of control from Moscow.[24]

Churchill's words described the new, postwar world and the interactions between East and West that became known as the Cold War. Unlike a traditional war, this struggle was fought behind the scenes, through political intrigue and influence, and it embodied many of the techniques that American anti-Communists had attributed to Reds in the United States for years. Like Churchill, they feared that the Soviet Union's newfound power and influence in Eastern Europe could expand into Western Europe, or perhaps to America. And while many eyes were watching the expansion of Soviet influence in Europe, others were seeing similar events in Asia.

Reds in the East

World War II had also featured fighting in Asia and the islands of the Pacific Ocean against Japanese forces. After Germany's surrender, Soviet forces defeated Japanese troops on the Korean Peninsula. A wartime agreement led to the division of Korea along the thirty-eighth parallel, with Soviets in control in

Chinese Communist leader Mao Zedong addresses his supporters in November 1944, when the Communists were allied with the Chinese government to defeat Japanese invaders. By the end of the decade, with the support of the Soviet Union, Mao and his party gained control of China.

the north and the United States in the south. A Socialist government administered the northern zone, while an American-supported government administered the southern zone.

Meanwhile, Cold War politics were also evolving in China. In the mid-1930s, Japan had overrun and occupied large portions of China. A group of Communists, led by Mao Zedong, were allied with the Chinese government against the Japanese. The government, under the leadership of Chiang Kai-shek, had been powerless to repel the Japanese invaders, and so welcomed Mao's support. However, after Japan was defeated, the alliance failed, and with the aid of the Soviet Union, Mao's army turned against Chiang's Nationalists.

Chiang's government was supported by the United States and received billions of dollars in aid; however, the Nationalists were defeated by the Communists in 1949. Mao instituted a Socialist government and lent support to the Communists in North Korea.

President Truman had been unwilling to send American troops to support Chiang's Nationalists. He and his administration had viewed it as an internal affair in which Americans should not take part; however, when fighting broke out on the Korean Peninsula, Truman viewed the events in a different light. This time, he committed American troops to the fray.

A "Police Action" in Korea

On June 25, 1950, North Korean troops invaded South Korea. The invasion touched off a storm of protests at the United Nations, which had been formed in 1945 to help mediate international disputes and to foster peaceful relations. The South Korean government petitioned the United Nations for help, and two days later, on June 27, the UN agreed to send a multinational force to combat the invasion.

President Truman called the UN response a "police action," saying in a news conference on June 29, "We are not at war."[25] The UN's intent was to return the situation to the preinvasion borders and defend the rights of South Korea. Truman's agreement to assist the UN cause sent American men and equipment from bases in Japan to help the South Korean forces, but once they joined the South Koreans in combat against the North Koreans, they became embroiled in the first shooting war of the Cold War era. The American and UN forces pushed the North Koreans back across the thirty-eighth parallel and then drove north toward the border with China. In October, Chinese Communist brigades poured over the frontier, destroying the advance and driving the UN forces south. The fighting was brutal and costly and eventually lasted three years before an armistice ended the shooting. North and South Korea were divided along roughly the prewar lines.

The Communist aggression in Korea was the latest example of what anti-Communists had been preaching since the first Red Scare in 1919: Communists could not be trusted, and they were aggressive, inhuman, and treacherous. In the years following the end of World

War II, their message was taken up by more and more American civilians and politicians from all walks of life.

Growing Fear and Suspicion

The postwar expansion of Communist influence around the world troubled many Americans. Republican politicians blamed the Democratic administrations of Roosevelt and Truman for the wartime agreements with the Soviet Union; they believed that allowing the Russians to liberate Eastern Europe had paved the way for those countries to become part of the Eastern Bloc. They pointed to Roosevelt's ill health; he had died shortly before Germany was defeated. They decried Truman's lack of experience; he had no international political experience when he became president. In their view, both shortcomings had enabled Stalin to mislead and lie to the Allies, which led to Poland, Czechoslovakia, and others to "fall" to communism.

In the decade following the end of World War II, the topic of communism was discussed daily across America. Media coverage outlined Communist repression in Eastern Bloc countries and attempts by Communists to overthrow other nations, such as Greece and Austria. Conservative newspapers and radio commentators sensationalized the news, with the repeated message that Communists could be anywhere.

There was little difference between these messages and those during the first Red Scare; however, mass media reached far more Americans in the post–World War II era. Newsreels shown in movie theaters and, more importantly, radio programs at home now reached more individuals than did newspapers. More and more Americans from all walks of life began to discuss the Red Menace at home, at work, at their places of worship, and wherever they gathered. The result was that additional groups began to take up the cause of anticommunism.

"Fight Every Foreignism"

Some of the groups that rallied to the cause of Americanism were well-established parts of American life. One was the Benevolent and Protective Order of Elks, or BPOE, which was founded in 1868. By 1946 the Elks had eight hundred thousand members in fifteen hundred centers across America. In July of that year, the

President Truman, left, meets with Wade H. Kepner, leader of the Benevolent and Protective Order of Elks, in 1946. The Elks were among several fraternal organizations that declared their commitment to preserving Americanism.

BPOE held their eighty-second annual convention in New York City. During the conclave, the outgoing president, Wade H. Kepner, pledged to the Elks in attendance that the order was committed to fighting communism in America. "We are going to fight every foreignism of any kind that attempts to come to our shores," Kepner declared, "even if it comes from some nation that was our Ally during the war."[26] Similar sentiments were declared by leaders of other fraternal organizations, such as Kiwanis International and the Knights of Columbus.

Other organizations were new on the scene and had been established specifically in response to the rising tide of anticommunism. Many of these new groups professed to ensure the preservation of Americanism and the exposure of Communists, their sympathizers, and their supporters (called "fellow travelers"). One of these new groups, American Action, Inc., was incorporated in 1946 to

The Smith Act

In 1940 President Franklin Roosevelt signed into law a measure called the Alien Registration Act. Popularly known as the Smith Act, after the Virginia congressman who introduced it, the law required all noncitizen adults to register with the government; however, one provision applied to citizens and noncitizens alike. It made it a criminal offense to be a member or an organizer of a group that was found to be "advocating, advising, or teaching the duty, necessity, desirability, or propriety of overthrowing or destroying any government in the United States by force or violence,"[1] or to be involved in publishing printed materials deemed related to such activities.

The act, which remains in effect today under 18 US Code Section 2385, marked the first time that federal legislation applied to thoughts of subversion rather than actual deeds. According to Yeshiva University's Ellen Schrecker, "What the Smith Act did that was unusual was that it made *teaching about* and *advocating* illegal—this is speech, and the Smith Act was perceived from the start to be a major violation of the First Amendment's right of free speech and association."[2] Nonetheless, the Smith Act was popular with anti-Communists during the Cold War and became the basis for prosecuting suspected illegal activity.

1. Cornell University School of Law. "US Code: § 2385. Advocating Overthrow of Government." www.law.cornell.edu/ uscode/18/2385.html.
2. Ellen Schrecker." The Rehearsal for McCarthyism: Anticommunism and Political Repression Before the Cold War." In *American Inquisition: The Era of McCarthyism* (sound recording). Prince Frederick, MD: Modern Scholar/Recorded Books, 2004, lecture 4.

inform voters across the country about candidates in the upcoming congressional elections. The company was chaired by the former national commander of the American Legion, Edward A. Hayes, who testified before Congress that the group planned to organize in every state to fight "all alien and anti-American groups that are attempting to destroy our form of government."[27] Hayes mentioned that his group had targeted candidates for defeat in six states. By October, the organization had received over $200,000 in contributions (approximately $2.28 million in 2011 dollars).

News coverage of such organizations suggested that the American public was truly concerned about the perceived threat of communism. The congressional elections of 1946 would measure the extent and depth of that perception.

"The Fight Against Communism Begins at Home"

One of the most important events in postwar America took place during the Congressional elections in the fall of 1946. Conservative opponents of President Truman, consisting of Republicans and southern Democrats, mounted political campaigns that proclaimed Truman was "soft" on communism. They accused him of giving in to Soviet demands, a practice they called "appeasement," which they believed would have dire consequences. For example, Senator Robert A. Taft, a Republican from Ohio, declared in a September 1946 speech that Truman's appeasement "only helped to build up

the greatest totalitarian state the world has ever seen. . . . We stand in danger of losing all the purposes and ideals for which we fought. This nation is in as much danger from abroad now as before the war."[28]

The danger that Taft and others saw came in three areas. First, they feared Soviet espionage in the United States; second, they were wary of Communist-inspired sabotage, particularly in labor unions; and third, they suspected Communists of subversion of individuals in American government as a result of working with Soviet representatives during the war, which might lead to changes in American foreign policy.

Republican candidates hammered their message throughout the campaign, playing on voters' fears of the Red Menace, which, given world events, seemed all too real. Their supporters went door-to-door to spread their message. For example, in the Eighteenth Congressional District in New York City, three hundred women banded together to support the Republican challenger, Frederick Bryan; in the words of one of the volunteers, their job was to tell voters that "the fight against communism begins at home."[29] The message hit home. In the 1946 congressional elections, Republicans won sweeping victories across the country, gaining majorities in both the House and the Senate. Clearly, U.S. voters were reacting to the issue of communism.

As a result, politicians from both parties took notice of public opinion. The Truman administration had begun an unpublicized effort to identify and remove suspected

Communists from government employment in 1945; following the election, Truman announced that efforts would be continued and stepped up. Some Republicans, however, were quick to cast a wider net in search of Reds to prove to the nation that they were, indeed, serious about the threat of communism.

"Our Job for the Next Two Years Shall Be to Rout Them Out"

Anti-Communists believed the 1946 congressional elections were a sweeping indictment of the Truman administration's policies, and they convinced conservative

politicians to join their crusade. For example, shortly after the election, a Republican congressman from New Jersey, J. Parnell Thomas, became chairman of the House Committee on Un-American Activities (often abbreviated as HUAC), which had met on and off since 1938 to investigate allegations of subversive actions and organizations. Now, Thomas explained, the committee had a new purpose.

In the recent election the American people manifested their deep concern over the inroads of Communism in the United States. They expressed a complete repudiation of

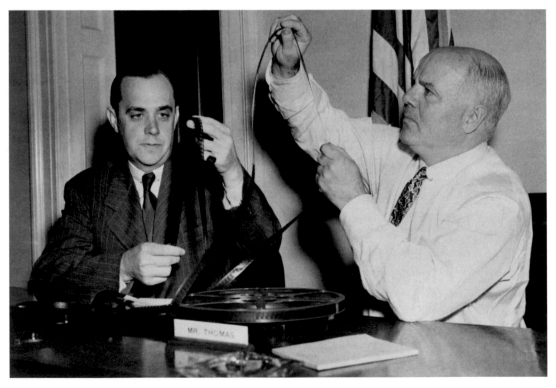

Chairman of the House Committee on Un-American Activities (HUAC), New Jersey Republican J. Parnell Thomas, right, examines film with a colleague as part of his investigation into alleged Communist activities among Hollywood filmmakers in 1947.

this encroachment from the left. They want no part of it. Nevertheless, we must face the fact that Communism has been operating under favorable conditions in the United States for the past decade. During this period they have succeeded in entrenching themselves in strategic and vital places. Our job for the next two years shall be to rout them out. This can be done by exposure, education and prosecution. The first two are the functions of our committee. The latter [is] that of the Department of Justice.[30]

Thomas's agenda echoed the three types of dangers perceived in communism by like-minded Americans: espionage, sabotage, and subversion. He vowed that HUAC would spotlight the role Communists were playing in American labor unions, examine Communist influences in educational systems and in the Hollywood film industry, and, most importantly, expose Communists and their fellow travelers in the U.S. government.

President Truman recognized that his administration needed to improve its standing in the volatile "Communists in government" arena. On November 25, Truman announced the creation of the Temporary Commission on Employee Loyalty, which was charged with studying the means by which the federal government determined employee loyalty to the United States. The commission was led by special assistant to the attorney general A. Devitt Vanech, who was a close friend of J. Edgar Hoover. Truman asked for the commission's report by February 1, 1947.

"Even One Disloyal Person"

The president's announcement came two weeks after the election. The commission's report was due shortly before the new Republican-controlled Congress convened. The timing of both the announcement and the deadline raised suspicion that the moves were politically motivated. According to historian and Truman biographer David McCullough, "The Republican leadership, having made communism a theme with such success in the fall elections, would keep up the demand for investigations, and Truman, to head off attacks from conservatives in both parties, had by this time accepted the view . . . that a program of loyalty reviews was necessary."[31] But at the same time, the president wrote to former Pennsylvania governor George Earle that he felt too much was being made of "the Communist 'bugaboo,'" adding, "I am of the opinion that the country is perfectly safe so far as Communism is concerned—we have too many sane people."[32]

Vanech's commission solicited input from about fifty federal agencies to complete its report and collected testimony from officials in the FBI and from U.S. attorney general Tom Clark. Clark believed that the number of Communists in the government was less important than the "serious threat which even one disloyal person constitutes to the security of the government."[33]

"Tail-Gunner Joe"

In 1946 former captain in the United States Marine Corps named Joseph R. McCarthy challenged incumbent senator Robert M. La Follette Jr. in the Wisconsin Republican primary. He played up his World War II service and began to use the nickname "Tail-Gunner Joe," even though the only times he flew during the war was as an unarmed observer. He attacked La Follette for not enlisting when the United States entered the war, even though the senator had been forty-six years old at the time. He accused La Follette of war profiteering, despite his own investments that had gained him thousands of dollars from war industries. His tactics worked. He won the Republican nomination.

In the general election, he faced Democrat Howard J. McMurray, a former congressman and strong supporter of labor unions. In Wisconsin, however, Republicans greatly outnumbered Democrats, and McMurray was the underdog. Because McMurray had been endorsed by the Wisconsin Communist Party, McCarthy questioned McMurray's loyalty and patriotism. Although McMurray repudiated the endorsement as well as communism in general, McCarthy's attacking tactics worked again. He was elected by more than 240,000 votes.

Clark had a long working relationship with the FBI and had lobbied Truman to expand the bureau's investigative authority. The commission was chaired by one of Hoover's close friends. Therefore, it is not surprising that its final report, issued on March 2, 1947, represented the influence and opinions of both the FBI and the attorney general. Its core conclusion echoed Clark's and Hoover's belief that the possibility of even one disloyal federal employee justified a comprehensive loyalty program.

Executive Order 9835

President Truman accepted the commission's major recommendation that all federal employees—some 2 million Americans—and all applicants for federal jobs undergo background investigations for evidence of disloyalty. Findings of disloyalty, according to the report, would be based on the conservative hallmarks of espionage and sabotage, as well as disclosing classified information, advocating the overthrow of the federal government, and "membership in, affiliation with or sympathetic association with any foreign or domestic organization . . . designated by the Attorney General as totalitarian, fascist, communist or subversive."[34]

On March 21, 1947, Truman signed Executive Order 9835, establishing the framework for the "Federal Employee Loyalty Program." All current and prospective federal employees were to be subjected to preliminary investigations called "name checks," using data from the files of the FBI and HUAC, as well as from former employers, associates, law enforcement agencies, schools, colleges, and "any other appropriate source."[35] If the name check turned up information that brought an employee's loyalty into question, a further investigation would be conducted by the "loyalty board" of that employee's department or agency. The employee would be informed of the board's findings, would have access to legal counsel, would have access to all materials associated with any accusations involved, and would have the right to appeal to a national Loyalty Review Board under the government's Civil Service Commission. Additionally, the Executive Order authorized the Attorney General to create a list of known subversive organizations for investigators' reference.

The executive order drew many favorable comments from members of Congress. Republican congressman Karl E. Mundt of South Dakota believed that "if the President's mandate is carried forward faithfully, it will tremendously strengthen the security of the United States."[36] Democratic senator Allen J. Ellender from Louisiana hoped that "every effort will be made to rid not only our government but the whole country of men and women who are in any [way] connected with any movement or any group whose aim is to overthrow our form of Government."[37] And the newly elected Republican senator from Wisconsin, a World War II veteran named Joseph R. McCarthy, said, "The

Loyalty Boards and Racism

Harry Truman's Executive Order 9835 mandated that all federal government departments and agencies, with the exception of the military, create loyalty boards. These boards were responsible for examining the results of the FBI's name checks and for investigating those employees who were suspected of subversive or Communist activity.

Some boards were more aggressive than others when dealing with their employees, and some were apparently more racially motivated than others. For example, during the Truman administration, the U.S. State Department had the lowest percentage of employees discharged from the government, and the U.S. Post Office had the highest. During that period, the State Department was largely staffed by white men and women with college educations, while the Post Office had the largest percentage of unskilled and minority employees within the government.

President Truman addresses a joint session of Congress in March 1947 to urge aid for nations at risk of takeover by Communist regimes. Earlier that month, Truman signed Executive Order 9835, which established a loyalty program meant to identify federal employees with ties to subversive organizations.

President's order certainly is definitely needed now, since over the past number of years there has been a tremendous number of communistically inclined employees on the Federal payroll."[38]

By the time of Truman's next press conference, former governor Earle had spoken publicly about the letter he had received from the president, and reporters wondered if Truman truly thought that "Communists in government" was, to use his word, a "bugaboo." He replied, "I am not worried about the Communist Party taking over the government of the United States, but I am against a person whose loyalty is not to the government of the United States, holding a government job."[39] Privately, however, he was concerned by the concept of a loyalty program, especially if it led to an expanded power base for the FBI.

"Not For Me"

Truman was not a fan of the FBI's methods or of Director Hoover. Shortly after succeeding President Roosevelt, he learned of the FBI's practice of tapping telephones, which his predecessor had permitted. Truman told the bureau, "I don't authorize any such thing."[40]

Roosevelt had allowed the bureau to assemble political information on Americans; Truman viewed this as a threat to civil liberties. Hoover had sent an agent to see the new president with the message, in the words of McCullough, "if there was anything the FBI could do for him, he had only to say the word. But having courteously thanked the young man, Truman told him to inform Mr. Hoover that any time the President of the United States wished the services of the FBI, he would make his request through the Attorney General [Hoover's superior]."[41] Truman later wrote in his diary, "We want no Gestapo or Secret Police. FBI is tending in that direction. They are dabbling in [personal lives] and plain blackmail. *This must stop …*"[42]

Now, almost two years later, Truman's opinion of Hoover and the FBI was unchanged. White House counsel Clark Clifford took notes during a conversation he had with the president in the spring of 1947 in which Truman was "very strongly anti-FBI … [and] wants to be sure to hold FBI down."[43] In a private letter to his wife, Truman commented that "Hoover's organization would make a good start towards a citizen spy system. Not for me."[44]

The president's reservations were well founded. Hoover's extensive files and information likely exceeded Truman's imagination. And it was clear that Hoover and Truman did not get along well. But now that the executive order had placed the FBI in charge of the name checks, Hoover was not about to let Truman get in his way in his anti-Communist crusade.

"The Protection … of this Nation"

Truman's federal loyalty program was, on paper, designed to ensure that the employees who were investigated had the same rights as other Americans under the Constitution. But the executive order put the investigations of 2 million government employees in the hands of the FBI, and Hoover's organization had a proven track record of conservative politics and anti-Communist bias that stretched back to the days of the Palmer Raids. Some observers, including some within the Truman administration, feared that the FBI might be too zealous in its loyalty investigations.

While the federal loyalty program apparatus was still being developed, Hoover gave the nation a glimpse into the bureau's philosophy and concerns. A week after Executive Order 9835 was signed into law, Hoover testified during a session of HUAC. This was an unprecedented move on his part, as he rarely appeared in person before congressional committees. In his statement, he indicated that "the aims and responsibilities of the House Committee on Un-American Activities and the Federal Bureau of Investigation are the same—the protection of the internal security of this nation" and that "this committee renders a distinct service when it publicly reveals the diabolic machinations of sinister figures engaged in un-American activities."[45]

Hoover's statement outlined how, in his view, the Communist Party had infiltrated many segments of American society. He reminded the committee that

Hoover testifies before the HUAC in March 1947, a week after President Truman signed Executive Order 9835. Hoover assured the committee of the FBI's commitment to the nation's security against Communist influences and alleged that Communists were active in many aspects of American society.

Communists remained at the heart of the labor movement and now was also entrenched in the entertainment industry. He proclaimed,

> The entire industry faces serious embarrassment because it could become a springboard for Communist activities. Communist activity is effective in Hollywood and is furthered by Communists and sympathizers using the prestige of prominent persons to serve, often unwittingly, the Communist cause.
>
> The party is content and highly pleased if it is possible to have

inserted in a picture a line, a scene, a sequence, conveying the Communist lesson, and, more importantly, if they can keep out anti-Communist lessons.[46]

If Hoover's intent was to demonstrate that the full weight of the FBI was behind the effort to rid the nation of Communists, he succeeded. According to Schrecker, "The FBI director's stature and alleged expertise ensured that the views he expressed in this statement received wide circulation. Politicians, journalists, academics, and opinion leaders of all political persuasions adopted his formulations and recycled them in countless speeches, position papers, judicial decisions, and magazine and newspaper articles."[47] And his assertions that Communists had infiltrated a wide variety of American activities were given more weight later that year.

The Attorney General's List

Under Executive Order 9835, the U.S. attorney general's office was directed to assemble a list of subversive organizations that the federal loyalty program investigators could use in their research. In March, Vanech requested that the FBI provide him with a compilation of suspected subversive organizations. Over

Despite his misgivings, Attorney General Tom Clark made public a list of subversive organizations compiled by the FBI and the Justice Department in 1947. The "Attorney General's List," as it became known, fueled Red Scare activities among the American public.

the next several months, Hoover's agency sent list after list of groups to be considered for inclusion before Vanech's office pleaded with the bureau to stop. By the end of October, Justice Department attorneys had studied 449 organizations; between mid-September and October 31, thirty-three attorneys were reviewing them full time, including some weekends.

The process had been kept behind closed doors. The Justice Department held no public or private hearings to consider the organizations' status; they did not give representatives from the groups an opportunity to explain what they did or what they supported. Attorney General Clark even considered keeping the final list under wraps. But because Executive Order 9835 was front-page news, he decided it must be made public, although he said in May, "We don't want this to develop into a witch hunt."[48]

In December, Clark released the list. It quickly became known as the "attorney general's list of subversive organizations," or simply the "attorney general's list." The list comprised over seventy organizations with dozens of subsidiary front groups and eleven schools. It received massive publicity. While the original intent of the list was to serve as an aid for federal loyalty boards during their investigations, it became much more. It not only served its original purpose, it also became the basis for other lists like it in the private sector. And, despite Clark's admonition, it contributed significantly to the evolving Red Scare that would occupy America for the next decade.

Chapter Three

"My Loyalty Was Constantly Questioned"

By the time the U.S. attorney general's list of subversive organizations was released in December 1947, the United States was firmly in the grip of another Red Scare. The dangers of communism were discussed daily in newspapers, on radio, in newsreels, on the new technology called television, and anywhere people gathered. A politician's career could turn on a single misspoken phrase about the Soviet Union, its allies, or communism in general. The federal government had begun an investigation into its own employees; private organizations wondered about the loyalty of their workers. American citizens wondered if something they had done or said in their past might contribute to how they were viewed at school, at work, at church, or among friends. They also wondered how much they really knew about their acquaintances, friends, and families.

Shortly after Executive Order 9835 went into effect, federal employees nationwide and at civilian government posts worldwide received loyalty forms and questionnaires to complete. All employees submitted their fingerprints and answered detailed questions about past and present affiliations, memberships, and relationships. The process of name checks was under way.

A name check was a straightforward but time-consuming process. FBI employees began by checking the bureau's vast index of thoroughly cross-referenced materials obtained from a wide variety of sources, such as military and police records, school and college transcripts, and earlier investigations going back to Hoover's first days with the bureau. The attorney general's list was the most publicized list of suspected subversive organizations, but for the FBI, it was a short list that was merely the tip of the iceberg. Their own files had many more organizations they considered suspect, and the name checkers delved into them as well.

The attorney general's list served another purpose that was perhaps unanticipated by those who initiated and created it. The list became an invaluable database for the rising number of Americans who started their own investigations. Some had been hunting for Communists for years; others were newly converted to the cause. But during the Red Scare of the late 1940s and early 1950s, they all had one thing in common: paper records.

Investigation in the Preelectronic Age

In the twenty-first century, finding information about individuals and organizations can be done from almost anywhere via the Internet. But before computers enabled users to save information electronically, anything important was recorded on paper. Both public and private organizations employed departments filled with men and women whose jobs were to handwrite or type everything from interoffice memos to annual reports. Mimeograph machines turned out millions of copies of church bulletins, union circulars, and group newsletters. Printing presses created millions of copies of daily and weekly newspapers and magazines, as well as legal documents such as deeds, mortgages, and birth certificates. These paper documents were everywhere.

The investigators of the mid-twentieth century began their work among these

The Paper Trail

Before photocopiers, e-mail, and social networking media, information that needed distribution was often reproduced using a mimeograph machine. A master copy of the document was created using a waxed stencil in a typewriter; the typist then created the document on the stencil, which, when removed from the typewriter, showed the letters and words as holes in the stencil. The stencil was then attached to the mimeograph's roller (or "drum"), which was coated with a special ink. Rotating the drum forced the ink through the stencil; at the same time, a mechanical feeder grabbed individual sheets of paper from an attached tray. Another rotation of the drum brought the inked stencil and the paper together, transferring the ink from the stencil onto the page.

Mimeography was widely used for all sorts of printing needs. It was a relatively inexpensive way to distribute newsletters and church bulletins. But it was also a gold mine for investigators, because unlike single-copy memos, which could be easily destroyed, mimeos left not only the dozens or hundreds of copies in circulation but the master stencil as well. All could be sources of incriminating evidence.

Workers tend to cabinets full of paper files maintained by the FBI in the 1940s. Before the computer age, investigators relied upon paper records, including public documents, newspapers and newsletters, memos, and other correspondence to collect their data.

records. Private citizens found that combing through daily newspapers, city libraries, local courthouses, and school or county archives was exacting work. It took patience and persistence.

However, few of these investigations took place in a vacuum. The network of anti-Communists that had been so effective in the pre–World War II years was still in existence. Investigators shared their questions, suspicions, and investigations by mail or in person. And starting in May 1947, they had a new ally in their cause, when a weekly newsletter began publication. It pulled no punches. It named names. It was called *Counterattack*.

"The Newsletter of Facts on Communism"

Counterattack was published by American Business Consultants in New York City and was financed in part by millionaire industrialist Alfred Kohlenberg and the Catholic Church. The company was founded by three former FBI agents, who had access to the bureau's thousands of anti-Communist files. Calling itself "The Newsletter of Facts on Communism," this four-page, typewritten weekly ran snippets of news stories on events such as labor strikes, union activity, or speeches given by radicals of any type. Editorials covered politics in the news, proposed legislation, and ways readers could take action. For example, when the attorney general's list was made public, *Counterattack* declared that the list was far from complete. The newsletter then listed thirty-four other Communist front groups that should have been included. Over time it ran the names of nearly two hundred organizations it considered front groups.

The December 19, 1947, issue contained a typical passage about unions and Communists (all spelling and punctuation is original):

COMMUNIST UNION AUTOCRACY IS SHOWN BRUTALLY in a new move by the [subversives] who control the huge CIO United Electrical, Radio & Machine Workers. The party commissar in UE is Jas J Matles, organizational director of the union. Number 2 man is Julius Emspak ("Comrade Juniper"), sec.-treas. The president of big District 4 (NYCity and NJ metropolitan area) is another Communist Party member, Jas McLeish.

A group of fighting anti-Communists are leaders of Local 1237, in NYCity. Its business representative, Jas A Conroy, was subpoenaed by Thomas Un-American Activities Committee several months ago. He answered its questions, telling what he knew of Communists in UE. For this he was reviled.

In the UE convention in October, when Conroy took the platform to speak, the Matles Communist machine gave him the booing treatment. This isn't spontaneous. It's a deliberate action on the [Communist] pattern to release & stimulate the sadistic instincts of the crowd, to destroy the nerve of the rebel who dares to stand up like a man, and to intimidate others in the hall who may have had notions of doing the same thing. . . .

Now the Communist machine is out to destroy Local 1237. If Matles and Emspak can't control a local, they'll try to disrupt it, smash it.[49]

People with union affiliations, including Congress of Industrial Organizations (CIO) leaders James, J. Matles, left, Albert J. Fitzgerald, and Julius Emspak, were typical targets of the newsletter Counterattack and other anti-Communist organizations.

Citizen investigators like the publishers of *Counterattack* usually had certain individuals in mind when they began their hunts. They began their searches looking for information that supported their theories. They believed that one person could be the link in a much larger chain of espionage, sabotage, or subversion. They suspected many union leaders of Communist activities. They also targeted those who advocated civil rights or the rights of free speech. And, in many cases, as with the snippets in *Counterattack*, there was little if any documentation supporting their accusations. The mere mention of one's name in such a context immediately led to suspicions of disloyalty. Hence, many leaders outside the federal government began to consider loyalty oaths for their own organizations to head off such allegations in their own businesses.

Loyalty Oaths in the Workplace

The postwar Red Scare returned union activism to the spotlight. *Counterattack*'s rhetoric was echoed by conservative syndicated columnists such as the *Chicago Tribune*'s Westbrook Pegler and the *New York Journal-American*'s George Sokolosky, and former Communists such as J.B. Matthews and James Burnham. They continued to insist that Communists could be found throughout organized labor and that Reds were working to unionize previously unorganized groups, such as California farmworkers, which would then become another segment of Communist-controlled labor. Their efforts brought national attention, and in the summer of 1947, their cause was given more ammunition in the form of the Taft-Hartley Act.

Many of the act's provisions were directed at the nation's unions. It mandated that unions create financial reports, prohibited them from making political contributions, and required their leaders to take an anti-Communist oath. President Truman vetoed it, believing that it was "unworkable" and would "discriminate against employees,"[50] but Congress voted to override his veto, and the act became law.

With the weight of federal legislation behind them, employers across the nation scurried to create loyalty affidavits for their employees and publicized their efforts to ensure they employed loyal workers. Sales representatives for New York–based business machines manufacturer Remington Rand, Inc. played up the company's repudiation of

"I Am Being Treated Unjustly"

In 1947 Samuel G. Whitney of Richland, Washington, sent a letter to President Harry S. Truman. Whitney had been employed as a construction worker at a nuclear power plant and had been fired by the Atomic Energy Commission for once having been affiliated with the Communist Party. Whitney pleaded with the president, "I am being treated unjustly by my own country. I am being accused of being a criminal without having had a fair trial according to our constitution. I am deprived of the right to earn a living for my family by my own government whose laws I have strictly obeyed."

There is no record that President Truman ever read the letter or even had it brought to his attention. Whitney's pleas went unheard.

Quoted in Ellen Schrecker. *Many Are the Crimes: McCarthyism in America*. Boston: Little, Brown, 1998, p. 270.

Members of the American Federation of Labor (AFL) rally in New York City in June 1947 to urge President Truman to veto the Taft-Hartley Act, which put several restrictions and mandates on unions in the wake of Red Scare-fueled suspicion of their activities.

a local union whose leadership refused to sign the company's loyalty oaths. General Electric, which had contracts to build atomic power plants from the federal government, assured the Atomic Energy Commission that its employees in the United Electrical Workers union were completely trustworthy.

Public employers also jumped on the loyalty-oath bandwagon. For example, in early 1948, Los Angeles County in California gave its twenty-one thousand employees a four-part oath to complete and sign. They were required to affirm their loyalty to the United States and the Constitution;

to disavow advocating the overthrow of the government; to list any aliases ever used; and to acknowledge any past or present membership in subversive organizations. At first 104 employees refused to sign, with the support of their local unions. After six months of contentious discussions, the county issued an ultimatum in July: sign or be fired.

Fired for "Insubordination"

The 104 employees who refused to sign the affidavit faced a difficult decision. Standing on the principle that the oath was an invasion of privacy or an infringement of the right to free speech was increasingly dangerous, because there was no guarantee that the oath would be declared invalid by the courts. Additionally, if the employee declared there were no affiliations, aliases, or questionable activities in his or her life, and evidence was found to the contrary, he or she could be imprisoned. Eventually, each employee reached a decision. Three resigned, eleven signed the full document, and seventy-three signed all but the final section, hoping that it would be found unconstitutional by the courts. The remaining seventeen were fired for "insubordination."[51]

Such predicaments were repeated across the nation. Untold thousands of workers were suspended or fired for suspected Communist activity. As they were not federal employees, they were not subject to the safeguards that President Truman had outlined in Executive Order 9835. They were simply let go. Most did not have the resources to fight their firings. Edward Lamb, an author and attorney who made his fortune investing in radio and television stations, was accused of being a Communist and was able to fight the accusation in court for years. In 1989, he recalled, "It cost me, first to last, more than nine hundred thousand dollars [in 1956, or roughly $7.4 million in 2011 dollars] to clear my name. . . . That's a sum that was far beyond the reach"[52] of those who were not as wealthy as he was.

During the Red Scare, the specter of loyalty oaths existed far beyond organized labor. Few professions in America were free of their presence. For their own peace of mind, organizations that hired or represented a wide variety of professionals discussed, recommended, and implemented loyalty oaths for their employees or members in order to avoid being labeled un-American. For example, the October 1, 1948, *Milwaukee Journal* quoted representatives of lawyers, doctors, and notaries public as being in favor of them for their professions. And one of the largest occupations in which this debate took place was education.

Loyalty Oaths on Campus

Anti-Communists were particularly suspicious of Reds in American education. They remembered that the Communist Party of the USA had been popular on college campuses during the Popular Front in the 1930s and had also been popular with liberals who supported civil rights. They suspected that the postwar American educational system could be riddled with these prewar members, fellow travelers, and sympathizers because, according to Schrecker, their assumption was that "Communism held its adherents for life."[53]

Indeed, some of the nation's educators had once been Communists or had associated with them; many freely admitted it. Some, like historian Daniel Boorstin of the University of Chicago, had joined the party for a brief time during college; others, like philosophy professor Barrows Dunham of Philadelphia's Temple University, had been members for several years before leaving the party. Such activities by a few individuals led anti-Communists to a broad-brush suspicion that former or current Communists could be teaching anywhere.

Many of the nation's educators were well aware of this suspicion. They believed that Communists had no place in the classroom but also believed that dismissing educators because of their political affiliations threatened academic freedom. Herbert Davis, president of Smith College in Massachusetts, declared, "I do not fear the influence of any extreme opinions in the academic world as much as I fear the attempt to stifle them and limit freedom of debate."[54] Dr. Robert G. Sproul, president of the University of California, the nation's largest university system, asserted in May 1949 that maintaining academic freedom was essential to safeguarding a college's integrity: "We would be well on our way to some form of totalitarianism whether we still called it democracy or not. I believe such academic freedom can be maintained even in a time of world tension."[55]

Sproul's contentions were put to the test later that year when the University of California's board of regents required a

Members of the CPUSA attend a May Day celebration in New York City in 1934. Americans who were affiliated with the CPUSA in the 1930s, especially educators, became targets of suspicion by anti-Communists after World War II.

loyalty oath from its four thousand faculty and administrative staff. It touched off a debate that drew national attention.

The University of California Loyalty Oath

The loyalty oath was introduced on June 12, 1949. Sproul's assistant, Dr. George Pettitt, declared, "We don't like the idea of oaths—nobody does," but felt the move was necessary "in the face of the Cold War hysteria we are now experiencing."[56] The oath read, "I do not believe in and am not a member of, nor do I support any party or organization that believes in, advocates or teaches the overthrow of the Government of the United States by force or by any illegal, unconstitutional means."[57]

The oath was unpopular from the start, surprising the regents. University systems in Michigan and Nebraska had implemented loyalty oaths without much comment or dissent. But faculty members throughout the California system objected. They pointed out that, since 1942, as part of their contracts with the state, they were required to swear to uphold the constitutions and laws of both California and the United States. They felt the new oath was an infringement on academic freedom and an unwarranted attack on their patriotism.

At the June 24 regents' meeting, a joint regents-faculty committee submitted a new proposal at that meeting. It read:

I do solemnly swear (or affirm) that I will support the Constitution of the United States and the Constitution of the State of California, and that I will faithfully discharge the duties of my office according to the best of my ability; that I am not a member of the Communist party or under any oath or a party to any agreement or under any commitment that is in conflict with my obligation under this oath.[58]

The first oath had not mentioned communism. Many found the revision more objectionable than the first. The debates continued.

"Sign Here or Leave the University"

California governor Earl Warren was well aware of the debate; he served on the board of regents. He felt the new oath was unnecessary, and since it was not required by state law, the regents could not even impose a penalty of perjury on a faculty member for taking a false oath. In April 1950, the regents voted to drop the "Communist party" clause of the oath in favor of inserting a similar clause in the employees' contracts. This new proposal was accepted by over 90 percent of the faculty and staff; however, more than four hundred refused to sign the new contracts, including forty-two full-time professors. Eighteen dissenters took the regents to court to keep the board from removing them for not signing the new contracts. In September, the California Third District Court of Appeals barred the regents from any suspensions, but the professors remained in limbo. They had not been fired or suspended, but they were not teaching either and had not been paid since June 30.

On December 22, 1950, the three-justice court heard the case. Attorney Stanley A. Weigel, representing the faculty members, claimed that the regents' action was an ultimatum that said "regardless of whether you have binding contracts, regardless of your conscience as a scholar or your conception of your duty to your scholarship you sign here or you leave the university."[59] Justice Annette A. Adams declared that since the regents were not accusing the professors of being Communists, "the issue then is that they were naughty boys and girls because they did not obey the teacher and sign."[60] In early 1951, the court decided the loyalty clause was unconstitutional and ordered the professors reinstated.

"We Believe the Decision Augurs Well"

The board of regents appealed the lower court's decision to the California Supreme Court. While the issue moved slowly through the courts, the human toll of the dispute kept growing. One observer noted that faculty members were increasingly demoralized by the fight with the regents. Employees were wracked with worry, depression, fatigue, fear, and insomnia, along with suspicion and distrust of their colleagues and a loss of self-respect.

The California Supreme Court upheld the appellate court's decision in October 1952, more than three and a half years after the original loyalty oath was proposed. Dr. Edward C. Tolman, professor of psychology at the university's Berkeley campus and spokesman for the nonsigners, was overjoyed by the court's decision. He issued a statement expressing "delight at the victory" and stating, "We believe the decision augurs well and happily for an end to the controversy which so sorely tried the university we love."[61]

Dr. Tolman and his colleagues were among the untold number of Americans caught up in the Red Scare mania of ensuring that all employees were loyal Americans. Their dispute drew local and national attention, keeping the issues and allegations out in the open. Other targets of the Red Scare were not so fortunate.

Loyalty plus Security

Unlike the situation at the University of California, most loyalty investigations remained hidden from view and drew few headlines. Loyalty boards worked behind the scenes, and with the beginning of the Korean War in 1950, their jobs took on a new dimension as the Red Scare entered a new and more repressive phase. The political implications of the war led President Truman and his successor, Dwight D. Eisenhower, to revise Executive Order 9835, in 1950 and 1953, respectively, adding the concept of national security to the loyalty program. Now investigators had a new standard against which they could measure suspect behavior.

Employees called before loyalty-security boards faced an increasingly wide range of questions to determine their degree of risk. In addition to questions about the individual's past or present affiliations, investigators asked about the Cold War as well. Typical questions included: Would you fight for the United States if it went to war with the Soviet Union? How do you feel about the war in Korea? Would you turn in fellow workers if you found out they were Communists? They also asked about social issues; black employees were asked if they had white friends, and white employees were asked if they had black friends who visited their homes. According to Schrecker, "One federal employee was even asked, 'What do you think about female chastity?'"[62]

A mail carrier walks his suburban route in the early 1950s. Postal workers were among a range of public and private employees expected to take loyalty oaths in the late 1940s and early 1950s.

The new issue of security provoked expanded investigations. For example, in 1950, the United States Coast Guard implemented a program to review workers who were handling West Coast ships and cargo bound for Korea. But after a few weeks, under pressure from employers and anti-Communist labor activists, the clearance procedures spread to ships headed elsewhere as well. Workers on domestic freighters, fishing vessels, and even passenger ferries became targets.

"He Was Given No Target at Which to Fire"

One longshoreman caught up in the Coast Guard loyalty-security operation was twenty-eight-year-old Californian Lawrence Parker. The Coast Guard's examiner told Parker that he was suspected of being a member of the Communist Party and was sympathetic to its doctrines but offered no evidence or specific information that might allow Parker to disprove the allegations. The best Parker could do was tell his life story in the hopes that the information he shared might somehow refute the unknown charges from the anonymous accusers. His attorney, Adam Yarmolinsky, complained, "Irrespective of [Parker's] merits as a marksman, he was given no target at which to fire."[63]

Parker's situation was repeated across the nation by the thousands. Both private and federal employees were suspended or fired without concrete evidence of disloyalty against them; the suspicion of disloyalty was now enough to label someone a security risk. In Philadelphia,

Arthur Drayton, a twenty-five-year veteran of the U.S. Post Office, was fired because he wrote essays and plays about African American history and because he had bought an insurance policy from the International Workers' Organization, which was on the attorney general's list. In New Jersey, Jim Kutcher, a decorated World War II veteran employed by the Veterans Administration, lost his job because on his loyalty form he listed that he had been a member of the Socialist Worker's Party before the war. Kutcher recalled:

At the hearings before the loyalty board, they asked me, "Did you ever use force and violence at any time in your life?"

I said, "Yes."

"Where?"

And I said, "In the United States Army."[64]

Kutcher was in combat for over a year, serving in North Africa and Italy. He was wounded in 1943 and lost both legs. Despite this service to and sacrifice for his country, he still lost his job.

Confronting the Accusers

Neither Drayton nor Kutcher held positions that had access to government secrets, nor had they performed any illegal acts. They were simply fired on the suspicion of being disloyal Americans. Like many who faced the loyalty-security boards, they were confronted with vague allegations from nameless sources. Kutcher appealed his firing to the highest level possible, the Loyalty Review Board of the U.S. Civil Service Commission. Each time, the allegations of disloyalty were unproven, but he did not regain his job. He recalled, "I was faced with the difficult task of disproving statements attributed to me by persons I couldn't cross-examine. The government refused to produce them. . . . Through all this, the government never produced any evidence that I ever did anything unconstitutional. But my loyalty was constantly questioned."[65]

This embargo on information handicapped both the accusers and the accused. The U.S. Constitution guarantees the accused the right to confront the accuser, but during the Red Scare, the guise of national security often made this impossible. Some investigators admitted they could not produce witnesses because they did not have access to that part of the inquiry; others declared that such information must have been kept secret for security purposes. Still others admitted that they were merely following instructions from the company's owner, the local school board, or some other, higher official.

In fact, the ultimate source of thousands of accusations against Americans was their own government. The FBI, led by Director Hoover's penchant for organization, amassed a vast archive of information on citizens stretching back to the days of World War I. And it was in the hands of the bureau that information was gathered, processed, assessed, and distributed to help root out Communists.

The FBI Under J. Edgar Hoover

By the time the second Red Scare arose, Hoover had been in charge of the bureau for over a decade. He was a master manipulator of individuals both inside and outside the government whom he believed were essential to maintaining the public's image of the FBI.

Hoover had spent the 1930s creating a network of allies in areas outside of the business of investigation. He courted the media so that they would show the bureau in the most positive light possible, such as for the effective pursuit of criminals during the Great Depression like John Dillinger and Al Capone. Hoover gave his favorite members of the press access to FBI information to help in fighting crime or hunting Reds; in return, the bureau received free publicity.

In his campaign against communism, Hoover ensured that the bureau was an active part of the anti-Communist network that had grown up in the 1920s and 1930s. He also took the time to cultivate a working relationship with members of Congress, particularly those who sat on the House's Un-American Activities

Blacklisting

Throughout the period of the second Red Scare, individuals who lost their jobs after loyalty-security board decisions or who were involved in congressional investigations discovered that they were unable to obtain new employment, not only in their chosen occupation, but in any field. They had been put on a so-called blacklist.

Blacklisting existed in several forms. The Attorney General's List was one; job applicants who were naïve enough to list association with any of the groups on it when applying for a job were turned down. A newer and more comprehensive blacklist appeared in 1950 when American Business Consultants (ABC), the publisher of the newsletter *Counterattack*, created a book titled *Red Channels*. It documented not only groups and organizations with connections to communism but individuals as well, such as authors and entertainers. ABC's writers and editors added many groups and persons to *Red Channels* with little or no corroborating evidence; merely being cited by a single source was enough to merit inclusion in the book.

Red Channels soon became a master blacklist. Companies discovered it was far easier to refuse to hire anyone listed than to risk the bad publicity that might follow the hiring of anyone on the list.

Committee. These allies believed in Hoover's fight against communism, but few if any of them were privy to the measures undertaken by the FBI in connection with Hoover's crusade.

Citizen Spies

One of the bureau's most successful tools in the anti-Communist fight was a network of civilian spies who believed that it was their patriotic duty to aid the FBI in its efforts. Their information assisted the bureau immensely and augmented the work performed by its personnel. According to historians Bud and Ruth Schultz,

> Being a professional informer emerged as a lucrative and ego-boosting calling for a special kind of person. James V. Blanc recruited his brother-in-law into the Communist Party and then turned his name over to the FBI. Barbara Hartle named both her former husband and a former common-law husband. David Brown padded his reports to the FBI with names of people he didn't know.[66]

One of the most famous citizen spies during the Red Scare was Herbert Philbrick, a former Communist enlisted by the FBI to infiltrate the inner workings of the party. His 1952 best-selling book *I Led Three Lives: Citizen, "Communist," Counterspy* was turned into a television series which ran from 1953 to 1956. Each script of *I Led Three Lives* was first reviewed by Hoover and the bureau for approval. The show and other FBI

Herbert Philbrick appears in federal court in New York City in 1949 after testifying against CPUSA officials. A former Communist himself, Philbrick became a citizen spy for the FBI.

propaganda demonstrated that the nation benefited greatly from the vigilance of Americans like Philbrick. Consequently, according to the Schultzes, "by 1954, one poll found that 72 percent of Americans would report to the FBI acquaintances they suspected of being Communists."[67] And the bureau acted on this information in a number of legal and illegal ways.

Dirty Tricks and Black Bags

Hoover had long believed that the Red Menace was the single most important threat to the United States. He was determined to eliminate this threat by any and all means at his disposal. His involvement in the Palmer Raids created a personal view of communism and radicalism that had remained unchanged since 1919. According to Schrecker, as Hoover was reading and collecting the radical literature of post–World War I groups, he was

> encountering American Communism at its most revolutionary moment, and that is the image of American Communism that [he was] going to carry through from 1919 [for the rest of his life]. In other words, [he was] viewing American Communism through this sort of post–World War I lens.[68]

Consequently, throughout the 1930s and 1940s, and particularly in the second phase of the Red Scare, Hoover felt free to use a wide range of illegal techniques when legal means failed.

Today, such methods are called "dirty tricks," and the bureau had many in its arsenal. One was the illegal wiretapping of suspected radicals. Although President Truman did not authorize them, the bureau continued the ones they had started under President Roosevelt in the belief that they were in the interest of national security, as well as instituting others. Hoover's agents tracked American citizens they suspected of illegal activity, and a hand-picked group performed "black bag jobs" of illegal break-ins of homes and businesses, where the agents collected or planted evidence in order to aid an investigation.

These illegal activities were far from the public eye. When allegations were leveled against a suspected Communist, few Americans knew how the bureau had obtained its information. And even then, the public or the accused did not get the entire story because of claims of national security.

Undercover and Under Wraps

Most FBI agents were plainly visible, working out of clearly labeled offices in cities across the nation. They gave speeches to schools and organizations about the bureau's role in the hunt for Communists. They visited businesses and college campuses to gather information related to name checks. But the core of Hoover's operatives was his corps of undercover agents. They posed as a wide variety of citizens in order to infiltrate suspected front groups, unions, and other organizations, and the information they garnered triggered further inquiries.

These agents' findings appeared in a variety of investigations. They passed information to government or private loyalty boards, but they did not appear at the board hearings so that the subject of the investigation had no chance to rebut the charges. Instead, the bureau's information was usually in a sealed envelope to which neither the accused nor the board had access. Both sides were only told that it contained evidence from the FBI. Agents also testified in court cases, but their evidence was given behind closed doors. Defense attorneys were not allowed to cross-examine the agents, so their testimony went unchallenged. The agents remained anonymous.

Hoover points to a map marking the locations of FBI offices around the country in 1943. Despite the FBI's public presence, much of its work under Hoover's leadership was done by undercover operatives who collected evidence that often remained sealed, even to the accused.

Protecting the Anonymous

This anonymity was demanded by Hoover in exchange for the agents' testimony. He contended that the agents needed to remain anonymous in order to protect their civil rights, but it also helped to conceal the dirty tricks that could have been exposed under cross-examination. Nonetheless, the climate of the Red Scare led many courts to accept the conditions without question. The courts believed their actions were in the name of national security. The judges believed that allowing such evidence assisted the bureau and the government in the fight against communism, although the testimony was both confidential and unchallengeable.

Still other pursuits of Communists in America took place on a much larger and more public stage, such as the investigations by the United States Congress, which brought the spotlight on suspected Communists across America.

Chapter Four

"Are You Now, or Have You Ever Been ..."

During the first Red Scare, the United States Congress held several hearings to examine the problem of American radicalism. After World War II, Congress played a much larger role as communism and its apparent worldwide expansion grabbed headlines daily. At the height of the Red Scare, members of Congress were household names for their anti-Red efforts. Their investigations were front-page news and were discussed on radio, television, and wherever Americans gathered. And their actions and repercussions affected untold numbers of lives across the nation.

Following the 1946 congressional elections, the U.S. House of Representatives moved to join the search for Communists in America. Its Committee on Un-American Activities was upgraded from temporary to permanent status. And in the years to come, the committee seemed to be drawing permanent attention to its activities.

Whittaker Chambers and Alger Hiss

Under the new chairmanship of New Jersey Republican J. Parnell Thomas, the committee, usually referred to as HUAC, heard from hundreds of witnesses about Communists in America. The hearings often featured former Communists speaking about past acquaintances, accusations of Communists in the U.S. government, and the behind-the-scenes presence of the FBI. One such investigation involved individuals who would soon become household names: Whittaker Chambers and Alger Hiss.

Whittaker Chambers was a former Communist who worked as a writer and editor for *Time*. He appeared before HUAC in 1948. He described a group of Communists with whom he had associated in the 1930s, many of whom worked for the Roosevelt administration. He testified that

the purpose of this group at that time was not primarily espionage. Its original purpose was the Communist infiltration of the American Government. But espionage was certainly one of its eventual objectives. Let no one be surprised at this statement. Disloyalty is a matter of principle with every member of the Communist party.[69]

According to the *New York Times*, "The charges made by Mr. Chambers . . . have rocked Washington."[70] Among those Chambers named, one individual, Alger Hiss, stood out from the rest.

Whittaker Chambers testifies before the HUAC in 1948 about his knowledge of Communist infiltration of the U.S. government.

Hiss was well known in Washington. From 1933 to 1946, he had worked for the Justice, Agriculture, and State Departments. During the war, he had attended the wartime strategy meeting at Yalta in 1945 and had played an important role in the creation of the United Nations. Hiss left the federal government in 1946 to become president of the prestigious Carnegie Endowment for International Peace. After Chambers's testimony, Hiss protested his innocence. He stated:

> So far as I know, I have never laid eyes on Mr. Chambers. There is no basis whatever for the statement he has made about me to the Thomas Committee. I have sent a telegram to the chairman of the committee to this effect and requesting that I be allowed to appear before the committee and make the same statement formally and under oath.[71]

Hiss's reputation was impeccable, and his voluntary appearance before HUAC two days after Chambers's testimony added to his standing. Members of the committee were stunned by Hiss's complete repudiation of Chambers's claims; South Dakota representative Karl E. Mundt declared that he had never heard such diametrically opposed sworn statements before. Only Representative Richard M. Nixon, a Republican from California, seemed unimpressed. In fact, Nixon insisted on digging deeper into the matter.

"I Was a Communist and You Were a Communist"

Nixon arranged for Chambers and Hiss to meet face-to-face in a HUAC subcommittee hearing two weeks later. Once he saw Chambers up close, Hiss recalled meeting him in 1935, but Chambers had called himself George Crosley. He also recalled subletting a Washington, D.C., apartment to him but said he had not seen him since 1936. Chambers denied this and stated that at that time, "I was a Communist and you were a Communist."[72] Because such a statement in a Congressional hearing was protected against a charge of defamation, Hiss challenged Chambers to repeat the accusation outside of Congress. Chambers at first refused but later called Hiss a Communist and a spy on a radio program. Hiss sued him for libel.

Chambers subsequently produced documents that he claimed Hiss had given him in 1938 to pass along to the Soviets. The documents seemed to contradict Hiss's statement that he had not seen Chambers since 1936. A grand jury called to examine the accusations indicted Hiss for perjury; the five-year statute of limitation on espionage had lapsed, so it could only indict him for lying under oath. During the trial, Chambers admitted that he had lied under oath about several events in his life, including when he had left the Communist Party. Hiss's character witnesses, including two Supreme Court justices, added weight to his contention that he had not been a Communist, and on July 7, 1949, the trial ended in a hung jury.

Richard M. Nixon

In 1947 Representative Richard M. Nixon was a freshman Republican from California, serving on the House Un-American Activities Committee (HUAC). Within a year, he went from being a political unknown to a household name, due in large part to his role in the Alger Hiss–Whittaker Chambers case. Chambers accused Hiss, a former high level government official, of being a Communist spy.

Nixon had not been swayed by Hiss's first appearance before HUAC during which Hiss professed his innocence. In fact, he had found Hiss smug and decided to pursue the matter further. The FBI gave Nixon information from Chambers's earlier bureau depositions, and this was essential in helping Nixon establish that Hiss had indeed known Chambers in the 1930s. He also discovered that Chambers had secretly hidden evidence related to Hiss's activities. The publicity from these breakthroughs soon made Nixon a household name.

Nixon was elected to the U.S. Senate in 1950 after an acrimonious race against incumbent Helen Gahagan Douglas, who Nixon accused of having Communist sympathies. Two years later, he was the Republican Party's nominee for vice president on the ticket with Dwight D. Eisenhower. After winning the election, Nixon served eight years as vice president. He lost the 1960 presidential election to John F. Kennedy but was elected president in 1968 and reelected in 1972. He resigned from the presidency in 1974 after his complicity in the coverup of the Watergate wiretapping scandal was brought to light. He is the only U.S. president to have resigned from office.

A second trial lasted from November 1949 to January 1950. Between the first verdict and the start of the second trial, world events took a dramatic turn that may have influenced the proceedings. Mao Zedong's armies overthrew Chiang Kai-shek's government, and the Soviet Union detonated its first atomic bomb. Subsequent public opinion polls suggested that Americans favored harsher treatment of U.S. Communists. During the second trial, Chambers's claims were reinforced by additional witnesses, and a new judge allowed greater latitude in questioning. The new jury found Hiss guilty; he was sentenced to five years in prison. Chambers was never charged with any crimes.

The debate continues today as to Alger Hiss's status as a spy or a Communist. But the significance of the case lies in the nationwide mindset it engendered. Anti-Communists' claims that Reds were in the federal government, even in positions of trust, seemed more plausible than ever. Additionally, the

Alger Hiss takes an oath before testifying at a HUAC hearing in August 1948 in which the former State Department employee faced charges of being a Communist spy.

case proved the significance of testifying before HUAC, and the damage that mentioning that someone was a Communist could cause.

HUAC and Hollywood

The House committee also investigated allegations that Communists had infiltrated the entertainment industry. Its members had listened to FBI director Hoover's testimony in March, 1947, and wondered whether it was true that Communists had succeeded in infiltrating and influencing Hollywood for propaganda purposes. To that end, the committee held hearings into these allegations in 1947, in 1951, and again in 1953, and

these sessions affected America for more than a generation.

The committee had a wealth of research and information available to them before the formal hearings began. The committee's director of research, Benjamin Mandel, was a former Communist and a member of Director Hoover's network of Red hunters. Consequently, the committee began their hearings with Hollywood professionals who were known to be sympathetic. These sympathizers started the process of naming names.

The 1947 hearings began in October with a week of testimony from actors, producers, and screenwriters. Familiar

The Hollywood Ten's John Howard Lawson Testifies Before HUAC

In October 1947, Hollywood screenwriter John Howard Lawson refused to acknowledge HUAC's right to ask whether he was a member of the Communist Party. After several minutes of rancorous discussion, the events reached this point:

Mr. Lawson: It is unfortunate and tragic that I have to teach this Committee the basic principles of American . .

The Chairman [J. Parnell Thomas] (pounding gavel): That is not the question. That is not the question. The question is: Have you ever been a member of the Communist Party?

Mr. Lawson: I am framing my answer in the only way in which any American citizen can frame his answer to a question which absolutely invades his rights.

The Chairman: Then you refuse to answer that question; is that correct?

Mr. Lawson: I have told you that I will offer my beliefs, affiliations, and everything else to the American public, and they will know where I stand.

The Chairman (pounding gavel): Excuse the witness . . .

Mr. Lawson: As they do from what I have written.

The Chairman (pounding gavel): Stand away from the stand . . .

Mr. Lawson: I have written Americanism for many years, and I shall continue to fight for the Bill of Rights, which you are trying to destroy.

The Chairman: Officers, take this man away from the stand . . .

Testimony before House Committee on Un-American Activities, October 27, 1947. Quoted in Albert Fried, ed. McCarthyism: *The Great American Red Scare, a Documentary History*. New York: Oxford University Press, 1997, pp. 42–43.

faces such as actors Ronald Reagan, Robert Taylor, Adolphe Menjou and studio owner Walt Disney named individuals whom they believed were either Communists or fellow travelers. Independent producer Sam Wood asserted that Communists in Hollywood were constantly trying to spread their influence and trying to "steer us into the red river."[73] These witnesses set the scene for the second week of the hearings.

"An Evil and Vicious Procedure"

Many of the screenwriters and directors subpoenaed to testify during the second week of the hearings had been named as Communists or fellow travelers during the first week. Ten of them cited their First Amendment right of free speech in refusing to answer the panel's key question: "Are you now, or have you ever been a member of the Communist Party of the United States?"[74] For refusing to answer the question, and for not cooperating with the committee's members, all ten were found in contempt of Congress. The penalty was up to one year in prison and a $1,000 fine (the equivalent of nearly $10,000 in 2011). This group soon became known as the "Hollywood Ten."

The Hollywood Ten had been prepared for an adversarial situation, but Chairman Thomas was openly hostile to them from the beginning. He interrupted them repeatedly. He refused to let them read prepared statements into

Supporters protest the prison sentences of screenwriter Dalton Trumbo and other members of the Hollywood Ten, who were found in contempt after refusing to testify before Congress in 1947.

the record unless he approved them first. However, Thomas did, grudgingly, allow one of the ten, screenwriter Albert Maltz, to read his statement. When Thomas asked to see the statement, Maltz asked whether another unfriendly witness who had testified before an earlier session of the committee had needed such permission. When Thomas noted that he had not been chairman during those hearings, Maltz pointed out that Thomas had been a member and could have objected at the time. Thomas was cornered and agreed to let Maltz speak. Maltz declared,

> For a full week, this committee has encouraged an assortment of well-rehearsed witnesses to testify that I and others are subversive and un-American. It has refused us . . . the right to cross-examine these witnesses, to refute their testimony, to reveal their motives, their history, and exactly who they are. I maintain that this is an evil and vicious procedure; that it is legally unjust and morally indecent, and that it places in danger every other American, since if the rights of any one citizen can be invaded, then the constitutional guarantees of every other American has been subverted and no one is any longer protected from official tyranny.[75]

The committee, the leaders in Hollywood, the courts, and the American public were not swayed by such warnings. The hearings continued. The ten were

confident that the courts would support their First Amendment rights and would dismiss the contempt charges. In the meantime, each found that he had been blacklisted and was unable to find work in any of the entertainment fields.

The Hollywood Blacklists

Shortly after HUAC declared the Hollywood Ten in contempt of Congress, the Motion Picture Association of America issued a statement about the group. It said that the Hollywood Ten would be immediately suspended without pay or fired and would not be rehired until they had been cleared of the charges and had sworn that they were not Communists. The group fought the contempt charges for more than a year before the U.S.

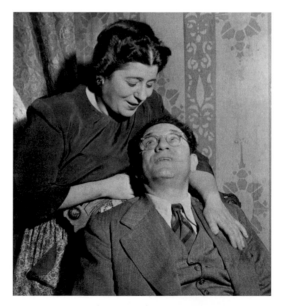

Philip Loeb, right, and Gertrude Berg appeared on the popular television show The Goldbergs *in the early 1950s. After Loeb was blacklisted, producers of the show replaced him with another actor.*

Supreme Court upheld the lower courts' convictions. Each entered a federal prison in 1950 for up to one year.

HUAC's 1947 investigation found no evidence of widespread Communist infiltration and influence in Hollywood, but it did affect the way the industry did business. The blacklisting of the Hollywood Ten was just the beginning; by 1951, dozens more professionals and personalities were on blacklists, both published and unpublished. Popular entertainers suddenly lost jobs as studios and producers bowed to pressure from advertisers and viewers. For example, fans of the popular television show *The Goldbergs* tuned in and discovered that the family father was now played by a new actor; Philip Loeb, the original father, had been blacklisted in the publication *Red Channels* and was fired by the show's producers who did not want to risk losing their sponsors. Even a cooperative witness could wind up on a blacklist, however. In 1951, actor Larry Parks cooperated fully with the Hollywood investigations but was blacklisted anyway.

By the time of the 1951 hearings, anti-Communist fervor in the United States was so strong that individuals who were mentioned only in passing became blacklisted, and the courts had decided that a witness's First Amendment rights were not sufficient for refusing to answer the committee's questions. Instead, those who were subpoenaed tried a different tactic.

Taking the Fifth

The Hollywood Ten's experiences showed that relying on the First Amendment was insufficient protection in the politically charged climate of the day. Soon, those subpoenaed by Congress began to rely upon the Fifth Amendment, which protects the witness against self-incrimination. But even that constitutional protection had pitfalls during the Red Scare. While the Fifth Amendment protected a witness from speaking about his or her own past or present affiliations, it did not protect him or her from the legal obligation of answering questions about others.

For Professor Barrows Dunham of Temple University, who had been a Communist Party member from 1938 to 1945, the Fifth Amendment seemed to be the best way to survive the HUAC subpoena he received in 1953. He believed that the whole business of naming names was abhorrent, stating,

> You can't name friends. . . . It's morally repugnant. . . . I had the sense that somewhere in my childhood I had learned that you don't tell tales on people, that you're not a tattle-tale. It felt to me as something laid way deep in my psychology. I couldn't do it no matter what. . . . And that made the decision easy.[76]

He answered questions about who he was and where he lived and where he had been born. He recalled that the tension was immense. "Physically, it felt as if I had an iron bar running between my ears. I was conscious of being in peril all the time."[77] But he refused to give details of where he worked and whom he knew, and the committee dismissed him after about ten minutes. Unfortunately, taking the Fifth did not protect Dunham from the university; it suspended him immediately after his appearance and fired him seven months later.

Others suffered similar fates. For those in the glare of the congressional spotlight, using the Fifth Amendment practically guaranteed a place on a blacklist because, as the anti-Communists claimed, it meant that the witness had something to hide. These witnesses were soon labeled "Fifth Amendment Communists." For Senator Joseph R. McCarthy of Wisconsin, it was a sure sign of guilt. He asserted, "A wit-

ness's refusal to answer whether or not he is a Communist on the grounds that his answer would tend to incriminate him is the most positive proof obtainable that the witness is a Communist."[78] And, beginning in early 1950, Senator McCarthy's hunt for Communists began to draw nationwide attention, starting with a speech in West Virginia.

"I Have Here in My Hand ..."

Since his election in 1946, Joseph R. McCarthy, the junior senator from Wisconsin, had made little impact in Con-

Ethel and Julius Rosenberg

Ethel and Julius Rosenberg became two iconic figures of the Red Scare when they were arrested for espionage in 1950. The FBI accused them of passing atomic bomb research to Soviet spies.

The case began with Klaus Fuchs, a German-born British physicist. Fuchs passed information to the Soviets while working for the British government during World War II, and in 1943 he was sent to the United States to assist with the development of the atomic bomb, called the Manhattan Project. There he passed on his atomic research to the Soviets through a project chemist named Harry Gold. Gold occasionally collected information from a project technician named David Greenglass, who was also passing data to the Soviets through Julius Rosenberg by way of Greenglass's sister Ethel, who was Rosenberg's wife.

Fuchs was arrested in 1949 in Great Britain on charges of espionage. He implicated Gold, Greenglass and Julius Rosenberg. Gold and Greenglass confessed their involvement, but Rosenberg refused, even when threatened with execution. The FBI then arrested Ethel, in hopes that her arrest would convince Julius to confess, although there was no evidence she had been directly involved. Both Rosenbergs proclaimed their innocence, but they were convicted in 1951 at the height of the Korean War. They were executed in the electric chair in 1953.

gress or in the Republican Party. In February 1950, the party decided to continue the anticommunism rhetoric that had been successful in 1946 and 1948 for the upcoming fall elections. McCarthy desperately wanted to be involved and begged the party leadership to let him help. While other, more well known Republicans were scheduled to visit large cities to drum up support for the party, the party sent McCarthy to Wheeling, West Virginia; Salt Lake City, Utah; Reno and Las Vegas, Nevada; and Huron, South Dakota.

On February 9, 1950, McCarthy spoke at the Lincoln Day dinner meeting of the Ohio County Women's Republican Club.

McCarthy's comments came just two weeks after Alger Hiss had been convicted of perjury, so his topic, the dangers of Communists in government, was fresh in his audience's minds. McCarthy stated that the United States was losing the Cold War because the State Department was filled with traitors and fellow travelers who were working for the nation's enemies. A significant portion of the background material and several of his phrases came from a speech Richard Nixon had recently made on the House floor. But the bombshell he dropped was the sentence, "I have here in my hand a list of 205 … names that were known to the Secretary of State and who neverthe-

Republican Joseph McCarthy casts his ballot with the help of an election official in 1946, the year he was elected to the U.S. Senate. He came to national prominence in early 1950 with his bold statements about Communist infiltration in the State Department.

less are still working and shaping the policy of the State Department."[79]

But he had no such list. He simply used a number based on a 1946 report of loyalty investigations in the State Department. The senator later said that he had meant to say that there were 205 bad risks in the State Department. At an airport stop at Denver, Colorado, the next day, McCarthy offered to show some reporters the list before claiming he had left it in his baggage on the plane. It was a delaying tactic, but it was enough to get the publicity going.

The Strategy

At his Salt Lake City speech on the tenth, McCarthy amended his claims, but only slightly. He said that in Wheeling he had "discussed Communists in the State Department" and had said he "had the names of 57 card-carrying members of the Communist Party" who were "the shapers of American foreign policy."[80] The number 57 was also based on old data from a 1948 House Appropriations Committee report. But the numbers mattered less than where these men and women supposedly worked and their role in the government.

McCarthy had hit upon a tremendously effective strategy. Instead of speaking of the dangers of treason, he spoke of the traitors themselves. In the view of journalist Haynes Johnson,

Not only would McCarthy speak of traitors. *He knew who they were. He knew where they were. He had a list. He had their names.* And the President of the United States and the Secretary of State knew who they were, too—or, at the very least, they could find out. They could expose, remove, and prosecute these traitors, *if they wished*, assuming they were not traitors themselves.[81]

The remainder of McCarthy's trip marked the beginning of what became his hallmark tactics: putting the responsibility on others to refute his charges, never answering challenges to his own credibility, continuing to make charges no matter where he was, and counting on headlines to keep him ahead of his critics. It worked. By the time he returned to Washington at the end of the long weekend, he was front-page news. Now his colleagues wanted to see his evidence.

The Debut of "McCarthyism"

After McCarthy returned to Washington, he discovered he had new allies that would help him bring his charges to the Senate. The Wheeling speech had brought him to the attention of several members of the anti-Communist network. In the words of Robert Morris, one of McCarthy's friends, "Here was a United States senator saying the same things they had been saying for years. They just embraced him."[82] They opened their files to him, and soon he had more information than he could imagine. The accusations of Communists in President Roosevelt's administration, the failure to support the Chinese Nationalists, the workings of front groups, the red-baiting of conservative Hearst newspaper reporters—more than twenty years of accusations and allegations of the anticommunism network was now at his fingertips.

On February 20, McCarthy addressed the U.S. Senate to outline his charges. His speech purported to document the Communists in the State Department; citing security reasons, he identified them by number only. In reality, he took a 1947 House report, changed the numbers of the individuals in the document, and made the descriptions more inflammatory. Suspected fellow travelers became actual party members. Relatives associated with front groups became dangerous security risks. More headlines followed.

The senator's accusations in the Senate, his style of rhetoric, and his accusations without corroboration led to a new word. A month after the Wheeling speech, *Washington Post* editorial cartoonist Herbert Block, who signed his works "Herblock," created a now-famous image: An elephant, representing the Republican Party, was being pushed and dragged reluctantly toward a tottering stack of buckets oozing tar, which was surmounted by a tar barrel and a small platform of wood. The elephant said, "You mean I'm supposed to stand on that?" The tar barrel was labeled "McCarthyism," and a new term was born.

McCarthy holds documents used in a speech before the Senate in February 1950 in which he outlined his charges that Communists were working in the State Department.

A Senate investigative committee examined McCarthy's allegations throughout the spring. Committee chairman Millard Tydings and his Democratic colleagues had believed they would be able to discredit McCarthy within a few days, but Tydings later admitted that they had let him "wander all over the map, out of Senatorial courtesy, instead of holding his feet to the fire."[83]

During that time, the Korean War broke out, giving McCarthy's allegations of State Department traitors more public support. The committee's Democratic majority voted to exonerate those he had accused. But for the senator, the committee report meant more headlines, more public acclaim, and a prized spot during the congressional campaigns that fall. The rhetoric now known as McCarthyism was heard by thousands as he stumped for Republican candidates nationwide. It led to more Republican gains in the 1950 elections. According to one observer that fall, "In every contest where it was a major factor, McCarthyism won."[84]

The U.S. Senate in the Red Scare

When the new session of Congress began in 1951, McCarthy was appointed to the powerful Senate Appropriations Committee. Among other matters, the committee oversaw funding of the State Department. But McCarthy's influence was not limited to one committee. A subcommittee of the Senate Internal Security Committee promised a wide-ranging examination of Communists in the government. They intended to revisit McCarthy's charges about the State Department and to investigate the military.

The military featured prominently in Senate business during the spring and summer of 1951. The Senate Armed Services Committee spent weeks probing President Truman's firing of General Douglas MacArthur over MacArthur's conduct of the Korean War and whether Truman's move could have been influenced by Communists in the government. Additionally, the Senate Internal Security subcommittee investigated what influence subversive forces might have had on American Far East policy. In particular, they targeted the Institute of Pacific Relations and the former editor of its magazine, Owen Lattimore. The Red hunters accused the institute of contributing to the "loss" of China, and McCarthy charged Lattimore as being "the top Soviet agent"[85] in the United States, which Lattimore vehemently denied. The Senate heard from witnesses who believed Lattimore had favored the Chinese and Soviet Communists in the 1930s and 1940s.

Senator McCarthy attended the subcommittee hearings. He sat at the table with the other senators, although he was not a member of the committee. Instead, he listened as an interested bystander. Watching the interplay of senators, investigators, and witnesses helped prepare him for his next role as head of his own investigating committee.

McCarthy in Charge

McCarthy was reelected to the Senate in 1952. For the first time in twenty years, there was also a Republican, Dwight D. Eisenhower, in the White House. The Republicans now had majorities in Congress and were eager to press their inquiries about and exposure of Communists in America. McCarthy's fellow Republicans acknowledged his growing stature by appointing him chairman of the Senate's Committee on Government Operations and its permanent standing investigating subcommittee. He promised that his campaign against subversives would continue.

McCarthy's crusade generated thousands of headlines for his investigating subcommittee, its investigations, and himself. Over the next two years, according to Haynes Johnson, the subcommittee

> initiated four hundred forty-five "preliminary inquiries" and one hundred fifty-seven "investigations." Of these, seventeen became formal, televised hearings. McCarthy led most of those himself. His purpose . . . was to expose Communists [and] fellow travelers. . . . Most of all, it was to generate publicity for McCarthy's anti-communist crusade—and for Joe McCarthy.[86]

He initiated more inquiries into the now-Republican-run State Department. He targeted Eisenhower nominees who spoke in favor of his political opponents. He also investigated State Department–run libraries overseas where local citizens could learn about America; the anti-Communist network suspected that the libraries carried works by subversive authors. The State Department eventually capitulated to his demand that thousands of books be removed from the libraries. Secretary of state John Foster Dulles later reported that staff at a few overseas libraries had actually burned some of the books in question. Such was the fear and power surrounding Josephy McCarthy in 1953.

The U.S. Army Hearings

In the fall of 1953, McCarthy looked into allegations of Communists in the U.S. Army at Fort Monmouth, New Jersey. The investigation began with his committee's request to see the army's confidential files of their loyalty-security boards. By early 1954, McCarthy's focus was on an army dentist named Irving Peress, who had been drafted in 1952 and then promoted to the rank of major a year later. The army subsequently learned that Peress had failed to mention a radical political affiliation during his loyalty-security review, and Peress's superiors were ordered to discharge him within ninety days.

When McCarthy learned of Peress's previous political activities, he subpoenaed Peress to appear before his committee in January 1954. Peress used the Fifth Amendment to refuse to answer questions, and McCarthy demanded that the army court-martial the dentist. When Peress received his honorable discharge from General Ralph Zwicker, his commanding officer, McCarthy was incensed. McCarthy's supporters and other anti-Communists demanded to know who promoted Peress; in fact, McCarthy knew it had been an automatic promotion based on legislation for which he had voted, but he chose not to publicize that. Instead, he summoned Zwicker to appear in February. During Zwicker's testimony, he insulted the general, a World War II combat veteran, calling him unfit to wear the uniform.

The senator's abuse drew significant ire from the press, veterans, the military, and senators of both parties. President Eisenhower, who until this time had refused to be dragged into the mire of McCarthyism, was also a veteran general of World War II and was incensed by McCarthy's comments as well. Early in his presidency, he had confided to his diary,

> Senator McCarthy is, of course, so anxious for the headlines that he is prepared to go to any extreme in order to secure some mention of his name in the public press. His actions create trouble [in Congress] with members of the party; they irritate, frustrate, and infuriate members of the Executive Department. I really believe nothing will be so effective in combating his particular kind of troublemaking as to ignore him.[87]

But it seemed as though the time for ignoring McCarthy had passed. Critics of his style and behavior were becoming more vocal with each investigation.

"He Dons His War Paint"

When 1954 began, Senator Joseph R. McCarthy's popularity was at an all-time high. Fifty percent of Americans in a January Gallup poll viewed him favorably, and only 29 percent viewed him unfavorably. But at the same time, there was a growing discontent among McCarthy's colleagues, others in the federal government, and in the media. They believed that he was starting to get out of control and that the nation needed to know about it.

As early as 1950, a select few members of the Senate had risen to speak about

General Ralph Zwicker, in his office, prepares to testify before McCarthy in February 1954 as part of an investigation into the alleged Communist associations of U.S. Army dentist Irving Peress. McCarthy's harsh treatment of Zwicker was criticized by his colleagues, the media, the military, and President Dwight Eisenhower.

McCarthy's tactics and demeanor. In July, Senator Margaret Chase Smith, a Republican from Maine, issued her "Declaration of Conscience" speech, decrying the rising tide of McCarthyism; however, only six other senators joined her effort and signed the declaration. In August 1951, Democratic senator William Burnett Benton of Connecticut declared, "In my opinion, Senator McCarthy has weakened the respect of decent people for representative government by his attacks upon the character of respectable citizens from the sanctuary of the Senate floor."[88] McCarthy replied with a personal attack, saying, "Tonight, Senator Benton has established himself as the hero of every Communist and crook in and out of government. . . .

Senator Margaret Chase Smith's "Declaration of Conscience" Speech

Senator Margaret Chase Smith, a Republican from Maine, watched Senator McCarthy's rise to popularity with trepidation. On June 1, 1950, she rose and presented her "Declaration of Conscience." It decried the current national climate, and turned out to be prophetic about the effects McCarthyism would have in the years ahead.

It is ironical that we Senators can in debate in the Senate . . . impute to any American who is not a Senator any conduct or motive unworthy or unbecoming an American—and without that non-Senator American having any legal redress against us. . . . Those of us who shout the loudest about Americanism in making character assassinations are all too frequently those who, by our own words and actions, ignore some of the basic principles of Americanism:

The right to criticize;
The right to hold unpopular beliefs;
The right to protest;
The right of independent thought.

The exercise of these rights should not cost one single American his reputation or his right to a livelihood nor should he be in danger of losing his reputation or livelihood merely because he happens to know someone who holds unpopular beliefs. . . . Freedom of speech is not what it used to be in America. It has been so abused by some that it is not exercised by others.

Margaret Chase Smith, U.S. Senate, June 1, 1950. www.usm.maine.edu/~rklotz/exhibits/smith.htm.

I call the attention of all honest Democrats to show how men of little minds are destroying a once great party."[89]

Opposition to McCarthy grew more vocal after his committees began a series of headline-grabbing investigations in 1953. Within a year, a number of his colleagues were tiring of his bluster and felt that he was becoming a liability to the Senate and to the Republican Party. Republican senator Ralph Flanders of Vermont was moved to speak against McCarthy after the debacle with army dentist Peress and General Zwicker. In the Senate on March 9, 1954, Flanders stated that he believed McCarthy was trying to destroy the Republicans "by intention or through ignorance" so that he could form his own "one-man party: McCarthyism." He also painted a striking verbal picture of McCarthy's behavior:

He dons his war paint. He goes into his war dance. He emits his war whoops. He goes forth to battle and proudly returns with the scalp of [Peress]. We may assume that this represents the depth and seriousness of Communist penetration at this time.[90]

Senators Smith, Benton, and Flanders were not alone. Many members of the media wondered about McCarthy's effectiveness and how it reflected on the nation. Their critical assessments of the senator increased in proportion to his presence in the headlines, and during 1954, they helped change American opinion about McCarthy and McCarthyism and ultimately about the Red Scare.

Chapter Five

Downfall and Aftermath

When 1954 began, the Red Scare seemed to have no end in sight. Anti-Communists seemed to be uncovering Reds everywhere they looked. But a number of writers and reporters had been working for years to try to keep Americans informed about the excesses and baseless accusations of the anti-Communists. These journalists focused on McCarthy's behavior when he became the most visible Red hunter. For example, Drew Pearson had been a long-time critic of the senator through his syndicated newspaper columns and radio broadcasts; McCarthy had even physically attacked Pearson at a dinner party in 1950 after Pearson commented about McCarthy's alleged income tax evasion. In 1953 Pearson's voice was joined by I. F. Stone, an independent journalist who penned a weekly newsletter that often took McCarthy and other anti-Communist crusaders to task. Even Henry Luce,

the publisher of *Time* and *Life* and a longtime supporter of conservative causes and anti-Communists, began to tire of McCarthy and ran editorials decrying the excesses of McCarthyism and the risks other politicians took in being associated with the senator.

One of the most effective means of exposing McCarthy's behavior was the emerging medium of television. At the time of the Wheeling speech in 1950, there were only 98 television stations and fewer than 4 million TVs in the nation; radio was still the dominant medium, with over two thousand stations and a radio in 94 percent of American homes. But by 1954, there were 35 million TVs in homes and 413 stations in nearly three hundred cities. Americans began to see McCarthy's brusque demeanor and his abusive questioning in Senate hearings for themselves. And one of the programs that brought McCarthy into American homes was CBS's *See It Now*.

See It Now's "The Case of Milo Radulovich, A0539839"

CBS's pioneering newsmagazine program *See It Now* was hosted by Edward R. Murrow, who had become a famous reporter for his coverage of World War II. Murrow introduced and narrated film segments, read news clips, and conducted interviews. By the fall of 1953, he and producer Fred Friendly wanted a story that would demonstrate more about McCarthyism than just what went on in Washington, D.C. They found it in the *Detroit News* story of Milo Radulovich's dismissal by the air force. They sent reporter Joseph Wershba and a cameraman to interview Radulovich, his neighbors, and other citizens of Dexter, Michigan.

Murrow and Friendly understood the potential dangers associated with such a program. There was a very real chance that it would land them on a blacklist. The program's sponsor, Alcoa Aluminum, was reluctant to run ads during the episode; the company made a lot of money supplying aluminum to the government and did not want to risk a run-in with McCarthy. To disassociate Alcoa from the episode's subject, Murrow and Friendly paid for a full-page ad in the *New York Times* to publicize the program, saying the content was their sole responsibility.

The program, titled "The Case of Milo Radulovich, A0589839," the number referring to Radulovich's serial number in prison, aired on October 20, 1953. It was a marvel of broadcasting. Wershba's interviews of Dexter's residents and the Radulovich family stood in stark contrast to the barbed wire fence and armed guard outside Selfridge Air Force Base, where Radulovich had been stationed and later interrogated. Radulovich's lawyer, Charles Lockwood, talked about how he had been denied access to the sealed manila envelope that contained the charges against his client, saying, "In all the thirty-two years that I have been a practicing attorney in Detroit, I have never witnessed such a farce and travesty upon justice as this thing has developed [into]."[91] Radulovich himself stated his case simply but eloquently; he said that he could not simply renounce his family connections in order to keep his job with the air force reserve. He asked, "If I am to be judged on my relatives, are

Milo Radulovich, an Air Force reservist who was dismissed from duty as a security risk because of the activities of his family, is interviewed on the CBS news program See It Now *in October 1953.*

my children going to be asked to denounce me? Are they going to be judged on what their father was labeled?"[92]

Murrow reserved two minutes at the end of the program for an editorial comment in which he stated,

> We are unable to judge the charges against the lieutenant's father or sister because neither we nor you nor they nor the lieutenant or the lawyers know precisely what was contained in that manila envelope. Was it hearsay, rumor, gossip, slander, or was it hard ascertainable fact that could be backed by credible witnesses? We do not know. . . . Whatever happens in this whole area of the relationship between the individual and the state, we will do it ourselves. It cannot be blamed upon [international Communists], or even our allies. And it seems to us—that is, to Fred Friendly and myself—that this is a subject that should be argued about endlessly.

He then concluded with his signature farewell: "Good night, and good luck."[93]

"A Report on Senator Joseph R. McCarthy"

Murrow and Friendly were unsure of how the program would be received. They did not have to wait long for their answer. Phone calls started pouring in to CBS; thousands of letters and telegrams arrived in the weeks that followed, with the vast majority expressing support for Radulovich and the program. *Newsweek*

magazine reported that the secretary of the air force's office received thousands more. Clearly, the broadcast had struck a chord with the viewing public.

The program remains a landmark in television journalism. University of Arkansas communications professor Thomas Rosteck notes that afterwards "there was, among the enthusiastic response, the sobering realization that a threshold had been crossed. The Radulovich broadcast represented a decisive step forward, taken by television to address issues sparking national debate."[94] Murrow and Friendly now felt empowered to take on McCarthy himself. On March 9, 1954, the same day that Senator Flanders stood and criticized McCarthy, *See It Now* presented an episode devoted to, in Murrow's words, "the junior senator from Wisconsin."[95]

In this program, titled "A Report on Senator Joseph R. McCarthy," Murrow let the words and pictures of the senator paint the portrait he wished to present. Simply saying where and when the speeches were made, he introduced clips of the senator at various venues, including in Congress. The program skillfully presented the case that McCarthy was a dangerous figure and that he was determined to pursue his personal agenda against all odds. Murrow's concluding editorial stated that American history showed that "we are not descended from fearful men—not from men who feared to write, to speak, to associate, and to defend causes that were for the moment unpopular." He reminded viewers that McCarthy did not create the Red Scare's

Newsman Edward R. Murrow offers editorial commentary during a March 1954 episode of See It Now *titled "A Report on Senator Joseph R. McCarthy," which presented McCarthy's activities as dangerous and self-serving.*

climate of fear and repression, "he merely exploited it—and rather successfully,"[96] and that the fault for allowing it to continue rested with the nation.

Accolades for this program exceeded those for the report on Radulovich. More than 9 percent of America's televisions were tuned to the broadcast—nearly 2.4 million homes. Americans were beginning to see the excesses associated with McCarthyism and in the coming months saw the senator in action as never

before. The U.S. Army was preparing to open fire on the man who had smeared one of its decorated soldiers, and their barrage helped bring McCarthy down.

Special Treatment

After the army endured McCarthy's insults to General Zwicker and accusations of the army's incompetence, they formulated a plan for retaliation. The plan centered on an army private named David Schine. This was the same David Schine who had served as an unpaid political consultant on McCarthy's staff and who had accompanied McCarthy's lead counsel, Roy Cohn, to Europe during the State Department libraries investigation. Schine was drafted into the army in November 1953 and was sent to Fort Dix, New Jersey, for basic training. But it seemed that Schine was different from the other draftees. He was excused from a variety of duties, such as cleaning the barracks or kitchens. He was allowed to ride in trucks when the other troops had to march. He was allowed to leave the base every weekend, saying he had another job in New York City that required his presence (although he was often seen at nightclubs).

In the spring of 1954, the army charged McCarthy and Cohn with pressuring the army to give Schine special treatment because of his connection to the senator; a leaked memo quoted Cohn as promising to "wreck the Army"[97] if Schine were sent overseas. McCarthy believed that the accusation was in retaliation for his questioning of General Zwicker earlier that year. The Senate assigned the task of investigating these charges to McCarthy's Permanent Subcommittee on Investigations. Karl E. Mundt of South Dakota, who had moved from the House to the Senate in 1948, agreed to act as chairman, since McCarthy, a defendant in the case, could not chair the proceedings. But the commit-

Roy Cohn and David Schine

During Senator Joseph McCarthy's chairmanship of the Senate Permanent Investigating Subcommittee, two of his most valuable assistants were Roy Cohn and David Schine. Both were in their mid-twenties and from privileged backgrounds and became household names along with McCarthy.

Cohn was an exceptional student who had graduated from law school at age twenty but had had to wait until his twenty-first birthday before he could become a practicing lawyer. He was recommended to McCarthy by J. Edgar Hoover on the basis of Cohn's work with the United States attorney in New York City.

Schine was the heir to a fortune from a successful hotel chain, and his hobby of studying communism brought him into contact with Cohn. When McCarthy explained that he had no budget to hire another assistant, Schine agreed to work without pay.

McCarthy dispatched Cohn and Schine to Europe to study State Department–run libraries. Their brash and smug demeanor toward the staff of the libraries and the members of the press generated headlines across the United States. They continued to work together until Schine was drafted into the army in 1953.

A family gathers to watch the Army-McCarthy hearings, which were broadcast live on two television networks and watched by over 80 million viewers in the spring of 1954.

tee agreed to let McCarthy cross-examine witnesses and testify himself. In the words of Haynes Johnson, "McCarthy was poised to act as advocate, juror, and judge."[98]

The Army-McCarthy hearings opened on April 22, 1954, and were broadcast live by two television networks. At a time when the U.S. population was approximately 150 million, an estimated 80 million viewers nationwide watched at least some part of the investigation. The most dramatic incident of the hearings came on June 9, when McCarthy leveled a charge against Boston attorney Joseph Nye Welch, who was serving as the army's lead counsel. Welch's reply seemed to give voice to the growing feeling against the senator.

"Have You No Sense of Decency, Sir?"

On June 9, Welch was questioning Cohn about a variety of subjects when McCarthy interjected with a new subject. He announced that a member of Welch's staff, Fred Fisher, had been a member of the Communist front group the National Lawyers Guild while in law school. In a droning voice, he wondered repeatedly if Welch was aware of this Communist in his midst. The cameras caught Welch leaning on the table in front of him with a look of deep horror on his face.

The look of horror was not due to McCarthy's pronouncement. Welch was well aware of his colleague's background.

He was reacting to McCarthy's breach of an agreement Welch and Cohn had reached earlier in a private meeting. Cohn had hoped they could avoid mentioning his draft status during questioning; two deferments meant he had not served in either World War II or the Korean conflict, and he did not wish to be portrayed as a draft dodger. Cohn later wrote that Welch brought up the Fisher matter, and the two agreed to leave both issues unspoken in the hearings. That night, Cohn went to McCarthy and told him about the conversation and the agreement; Cohn wrote in his memoirs, "McCarthy approved the trade."[99]

Now McCarthy had broken his promise to Cohn. Once McCarthy had finished, Welch began to defend Fisher and laid out in a tired but firm voice his knowledge of Fisher's background, his fear that Fisher's former activities would hurt him in the future, and that McCarthy's attempted smear might hurt him in the present. Welch stated, "Let us not assassinate this lad further, senator. You have done enough. Have you no sense of decency, sir, at long last? Have you left no sense of decency?"[100]

McCarthy launched into another attack, this time connecting Welch's questioning of Cohn and the Fisher issue, but Welch had the final word, dropping the honorific "Senator" when he addressed McCarthy:

Mr. McCarthy, I will not discuss this further with you. You have sat within six feet of me, and could have asked me about Fred Fisher.

U.S. Army counsel Senator Joseph Welch reacts in disgust to a verbal attack by McCarthy during the Army-McCarthy hearings in June 1954.

You have seen fit to bring it out, and if there is a God in heaven, it will do neither you nor your cause any good. I will not discuss it further. I will not ask Mr. Cohn any more questions. You, Mr. Chairman, may, if you will, call the next witness.[101]

Chairman Mundt asked whether there were any more questions, and there was silence from the committee and in the hearing room. Then suddenly the room erupted with the thunderous din of applause. Mundt declared a recess and left the room. Welch rose stiffly and walked out, looking close to tears. McCarthy followed, looking grim; he recognized that he had been dealt a blow, but did not seem to understand why. He was surrounded by people in the outer hallway, and he kept asking, "What did I do? What did I do?"[102] The answer was that he had set in motion his own destruction.

"To Bring the Senate into Disrepute"

The Army-McCarthy hearings slogged on for another week. But the American public's view of Senator McCarthy was never the same again. They had seen firsthand his bullying, his vindictiveness, and his arrogance, and his approval ratings dropped sharply. His 50 percent approval rating in January 1954 dropped to 34 percent in June; additionally, those with a negative opinion of him climbed during the same period from 29 to 45 percent.

The hearings also convinced many senators that McCarthy was a liability to the Senate's reputation. On June 11, Senator Flanders introduced a motion that accused McCarthy of conduct "contrary to senatorial traditions," that tended "to bring the Senate into disrepute," and that "such conduct is hereby condemned."[103] He also recommended that McCarthy be stripped of his committee chairmanship positions.

In August, vice president Richard Nixon, as president of the Senate, appointed three Republicans and three Democrats to investigate forty-six charges against McCarthy, ranging from his refusal to cooperate with a committee investigating his alleged income tax evasion to his abuse of General Zwicker. He asked Republican Arthur Watkins of Utah to serve as committee chairman.

"Just A Minute, Senator"

By October the Watkins Committee had diligently whittled the charges against McCarthy down to five. While Watkins allowed McCarthy to attend the meetings and defend himself, he refused to let McCarthy conduct business as he was accustomed to doing. According to Harry Johnston of *Life*, "[Watkins] did not hesitate at the very beginning to silence McCarthy's attempted interruptions with an unrelenting gavel. As McCarthy tried time after time his old, hitherto effective tactics of wild diversion, Watkins usually cut him off with a decorous but devastatingly icy 'Just a minute, Senator.'"[104] The committee recommended that McCarthy be censured as outlined in Senator Flanders's motion.

In November, the full Senate took up the Watkins Committee's recommendations and reduced the charges to two.

The tax evasion issue and the Zwicker incident remained until the latter was replaced with a charge of contempt related to the Watkins Committee. On December 2, 1954, the Senate voted sixty-seven to twenty-two to condemn McCarthy on both counts. Every Democratic senator present voted in favor, along with twenty-two Republicans. McCarthy's supporters claimed that the rebuke was less formal or critical than a censure because the final report had used the word *condemn*, but one senator, reading the dictionary's definitions of both words, proclaimed that he thought *condemn* was stronger than *censure*.

Regardless of the wording or the definitions, McCarthy's influence was destroyed. He lost his chairmanship positions, and colleagues no longer solicited his opinions or attended his speeches on the Senate floor. Perhaps the worst consequence for McCarthy, who

Senator Ralph Flanders reads a newspaper account of the Watkins Committee's recommendation to censure McCarthy in the fall of 1954.

sought and loved the attention of the media, was that reporters no longer listened to him, and his name disappeared from the headlines.

"Mere Unorthodoxy or Dissent . . . Is Not to Be Condemned"

The Red Scare, however, did not end with McCarthy's downfall, although its most visible figure no longer made news. Instead, many of the headlines related to anti-Communist crusades now came from the courts. Former California governor Earl Warren, who had been involved in the University of California loyalty-oath issue, was appointed Chief Justice of the United States by President Eisenhower in 1953. Under his leadership, the Supreme Court examined a number of Red Scare–related cases and issued a number of decisions that supported an individual's rights concerning the nation's loyalty and security programs.

Two important decisions came in 1956. In the case of *Mesarosh v. United States*, the Court rebuked the government prosecutors for pursuing a conviction under the 1940 Smith Act by relying on paid FBI informants with unreliable backgrounds. The decision affirmed that "the dignity of the United States Government will not permit the conviction of any person by tainted testimony."[105] In *Cole v. Young*, the Court clarified the use of the undefined "national security" standard that had existed since 1950. It held that the government could not justify applying high-level loyalty-security standards to all government employees. This helped eliminate the practice of dismissal through guilt by association that had been a hallmark of the Red Scare. The Court's decisions led to a significant decrease in federal government loyalty-security investigations of civilians; by 1962, they were virtually nonexistent.

In 1957's *Sweezy v. New Hampshire*, the Court overturned the contempt conviction of a University of New Hampshire professor who had lost his job due to past affiliations, affirming that "mere unorthodoxy or dissent from the prevailing mores is not to be condemned. The absence of such voices would be a symptom of grave illness in our society."[106] The decision was a victory for academic freedom and another defeat for the practice of guilt by association.

While the Supreme Court deliberated *Sweezy v. New Hampshire*, Senator McCarthy returned to the headlines, only this time under much different circumstances. In the three years following the Senate vote, he had fallen into ill health.

"A Figure Out of the Past"

McCarthy had been out of the public eye for years. He had made a few public appearances, but the crowds were a mere shadow of what they had once been. For example, organizers of a "McCarthy Day" in Boscobel, Wisconsin, in 1955 predicted a crowd of fifty thousand; actual attendance was fifteen hundred. Although still a United States senator, he rarely visited his office, preferring to remain at home. His consumption of alcohol, which had been significant during the height of his power, had increased to troubling levels. His wife, Jean, a former staff researcher whom he had married in 1953, tried to convince him he needed help and medical treatment and enlisted his remaining close friends to convince him to stop drinking. It was too late, however; McCarthy entered Bethesda Naval Hospital on April 28, 1957, and died there on May 2 with his wife and a priest by his side. He was forty-eight years old. The official cause of death was the liver disease hepatitis, although some contemporary observers believed that he had drunk himself to death.

He lay in state in the Senate and in his home town of Appleton, Wisconsin, where hundreds lined up to pay their respects. His funeral was attended by several senators, and he was buried next to his parents in a cemetery overlooking the Fox River. By the time of his death, the nation had moved beyond the worst of the Red Scare. The Korean War was over, communism seemed to be in check worldwide, and the threat of atomic war with the Soviet Union seemed less likely. As *Life* magazine put it, "When he died last week, Joe McCarthy already seemed a figure out of the past."[107]

While Joseph R. McCarthy was the most visible and most colorful figure of the Red Scare era, the campaign against suspected Communists in the United States did not end with his death. FBI director Hoover continued his crusade against them, as well as anyone he suspected of subversion, with much less fanfare until his own death in 1972. He had been director for thirty-seven years and had served eight presidents. In his

Marines carry McCarthy's casket at his funeral in Appleton, Wisconsin, in May 1957. By the time of the senator's death, the Red Scare in United States was largely over.

wake were untold numbers of investigations and countless victims.

The Victims Left Behind

It is unlikely that the number of victims created by the Red Scare will ever be known. As Schrecker notes, "The literature of the McCarthy era abounds with stories of former friends crossing the street to avoid having to greet unfriendly witnesses and [of] insurance companies refusing to write policies for government employees who lost their jobs. Such manifestations of anxiety were extreme, but not entirely unrealistic."[108] It is true that many men and women left or lost their jobs for valid reasons; some had been Communists and had performed questionable or illegal acts. But they were few in number compared with those who lost their jobs due to loyalty-security board investigations, antiunion employers, or blacklists, not to mention the husbands, wives, children, friends, and relatives who shared their burden of fear, depression, and despair.

The easing of the Red Scare in the mid-1950s meant that some individuals could return to the jobs from which they had been fired. Jim Kutcher, who had lost both his legs serving his country during World War II but was deemed a security risk by the Veterans Administration, was reinstated, with back pay, in 1958, eight years after he was fired. Arthur Drayton, the post office employee with twenty-five years of service before his suspension in 1948, was reinstated in 1950, only to be suspended again in 1953. After the Supreme Court decision in *Cole v. Young* in 1956, he was reinstated a second time, and retired from the post office in 1959.

Other victims found it harder to return to their original occupations. The members of the Hollywood Ten served their prison sentences but remained blacklisted for years. Some were able to find work overseas; others wrote under assumed names. For example, Dalton Trumbo wrote under the pseudonym Robert Rich and won an Oscar for 1956's *The Brave One*, which marked the beginning of the end of the blacklist. But Barrows Dunham, the Temple University professor, had to wait fifteen years before the university relented and let him teach again.

Milo Radulovich, however, was just starting his professional life when he was caught up in the Red Scare. His fame turned out to be a mixed blessing.

Milo Radulovich

The Red Scare and Edward R. Murrow's *See It Now* had made Milo Radulovich a household name for a short time in 1953. The episode brought an outpouring of public support for his case. A week after the program aired, Murrow reported that the secretary of the air force, Harold E. Talbott, had agreed to review Radulovich's case. Radulovich was reinstated less than a month later; however, he had a difficult time finding a job and seemed to be on an unofficial blacklist.

His marriage broke up, and he moved to California, hoping for a new start. He eventually found a job in meteorology with a small company before moving to the National Weather Service in the 1970s. Working out of the Sacramento office, he often served as a spokesman for weather conditions across the state; reporters who quoted him either did not know of his connection to the Red Scare or chose not to mention it. Even an article highlighting his forecasting associated with the landmark 1988 Yellowstone National Park wildfires failed to mention his brush with fame thirty-five years earlier.

Radulovich retired in 1994, and in 2001 moved to Lodi, California. He led a quiet life until he was approached by actor George Clooney to serve as a consultant on *Good Night, and Good Luck,* Clooney's dramatization of the *See It Now* McCarthy broadcasts. After the film's success, Radulovich found himself in demand as a public speaker and became active in social justice causes, such as freedom of speech and freedom of the press. He died in November 2007.

Milestones

By the time Milo Radulovich passed away, most of the other figures of the Red Scare were long deceased, and the era was a distant memory. Alger Hiss died in 1996 at age ninety, continuing to proclaim he had not been a spy. His nemesis, Whittaker Chambers, died of a heart attack in 1961 at the age of sixty. Richard M. Nixon died in 1994, having been elected president of the United States in 1968 and 1972 before resigning in disgrace in the wake of the Watergate scandal in 1974. David Schine went on to a career in music production and engineering and died along with his wife and one of his sons in a private airplane crash in 1996. Roy Cohn also left politics and went into private law practice in New York City; he died of complications from AIDS in 1986.

Edward R. Murrow won two Emmys for his television work before leaving CBS in 1960; he died of lung cancer in 1965. His producer, Fred Friendly, who left CBS to help create the Public Broadcasting System, died in 1998. Joseph Wershba, the reporter who conducted the interviews in "The Case of Milo Radulovich, A0539839," outlived them all. He later worked for twenty years as a producer for CBS's long-running newsmagazine *60 Minutes* until his retirement in 1988. He died in 2011.

The Soviet Union also passed into history. The fear of Communist expansion

A statue of Lenin that had been toppled by protesters during the events leading to the break up of the Soviet Union, is loaded onto a truck in Lithuania in August 1991.

Joseph Wershba

In the fall of 1953, Joseph Wershba was a reporter and producer for CBS News, working with Edward R. Murrow and Fred Friendly on the *See It Now* program. Murrow and Friendly dispatched Wershba to Michigan to interview Milo Radulovich and Radulovich's neighbors, friends, and family for the episode that helped put a face on the impact and consequences of the Red Scare.

While Murrow and Friendly were the public faces of *See It Now*, Wershba was one of the key players behind the scenes, interviewing newsmakers and crafting film segments. He later served as one of the original producers of CBS's pioneering newsmagazine *60 Minutes* when it debuted in 1968. He won two Emmy Awards for his work on the program. He retired from CBS in 1988.

When Wershba died on May 14, 2011, Jeff Fager, chairman of CBS News, remembered Wershba as "a wonderful man who was a pioneer of broadcast journalism."[1] Former CBS reporter Marvin Kalb said Wershba "resented small people being caught in . . . the grinding wheels of [politics] in Washington. He had an instinct against phoniness and an arbitrary use of power."[2]

1. Quoted in BBC News Entertainment & Arts. "News Pioneer Joseph Wershba Dies at 90," May 17, 2011. www.bbc.co.uk/news/entertainment-arts-13422098.
2. Quoted in Emma Brown. "Joseph Wershba, CBS Producer and '60 Minutes' Mainstay, Dies at 90." *Washington Post*, May 16, 2011. www.washingtonpost.com/local/obituaries/joseph-wershba/2011/05/16/AF3keF5G_story.html.

ebbed and flowed during the rest of the twentieth century, but the fear of all-out atomic war with the Soviets diminished in the 1970s as American and Russian diplomats and politicians discussed and signed nuclear test ban and disarmament treaties. In the 1980s, Soviet premier Mikhail Gorbachev helped lead his nation toward a more open society while citizens in the Soviet Bloc countries began to break away from Soviet control. In 1991, the Soviet Union broke up, to be replaced by the current Russian Federation and a myriad of newly independent states across Central Asia. The Soviet Bloc disappeared as well, as Churchill's "Iron Curtain" dissolved amidst movements of democracy and nationalism.

Today, many Russians who grew up in the 1980s refer to the pre-Gorbachev era with the phrase "in Soviet times," as a way of recalling a bygone era that they hope does not return. In the United States, the term "Red Scare" also recalls a bygone era, but it has also been adopted by sports teams and at least one group of musicians. The term no longer has the threat of national destruction by unseen and insidious forces that it had in the twentieth century.

An Incomplete Legacy

As the Red Scare faded, it took many Americans a decade or more to put the era behind them. Schools and universities were affected nationwide; Schrecker notes that "a silent generation of students populated the nation's campuses, while their professors shrank from anything that might be construed as controversial . . . and meaningful political dissent had all but withered away."[109] This timidity remained the status quo until the political and social upheavals of the mid- to late 1960s. The fear of blacklisting continued to hang over the entertainment industries as well, as television and films steered away from emerging controversial topics, such as race relations and equal rights for minorities and women.

Although the era of McCarthyism is several decades in the past, and the first Red Scare is nearly a century old, the legacy of both remain incomplete. Many Americans who lived through McCarthyism do not wish to discuss it, and researchers remain stymied by court decisions that keep records sealed under the guise of privacy. For example, in May 2011, historian Lisa Harbatkin, whose educator parents were blacklisted by New York City's Board of Education,

"Hooverism" Instead of "McCarthyism"?

Given the high visibility and widespread publicity surrounding the height of Senator McCarthy's career, it is perhaps expected that the term "McCarthyism" has been applied to the most repressive portion of the second Red Scare since the post–World War II attitudes and anti-Soviet propaganda that helped shape the Cold War were substantially the same as those that existed in the 1920s and 1930s. This has led some historians to suggest that a better term would be "Hooverism," as it would embrace the entire era of the twentieth-century Red Scare.

While J. Edgar Hoover did not initiate the Red Scare, he was perhaps its driving force. In the years when anti-Red fervor was low, Hoover maintained his contacts with the anticommunism network, encouraged their efforts, and ensured that all the pieces were in place if they were needed to fight communism in America again. And when McCarthy decided to take on the issue of Communists in government, Hoover was only too happy to connect him to the existing anti-Red network and to supply him with confidential information to assist the senator's investigations.

was denied access to loyalty board investigations of more than one thousand public school teachers. An appellate court decided that giving Harbatkin unrestricted access to the records without the consent of those investigated or their descendants would result in an invasion of their privacy.

The U.S. government seems to feel likewise. Although the FBI has opened its files for public scrutiny, not every FBI file is accessible, including those related to current investigations. Americans can now discover what records exist in the bureau's archives about themselves or their relatives, but sometimes what they receive contains blacked out passages of information deemed important to national security. Additionally, although the House Committee on Un-American Activities ceased operation in 1975, the complete records of the committee's actions remain sealed. They will be unavailable to the public until 2026 at the earliest. Perhaps at that time, a more complete history of the Red Scare can be written.

Notes

Chapter One: The Rise of the "Reds"

1. Quoted in W. Bruce Lincoln. *Red Victory: A History of the Russian Civil War.* New York: Simon & Schuster, 1989, p. 29.
2. Barbara W. Tuchman. *The Proud Tower: A Portrait of the World Before the War, 1890–1914.* New York: Macmillan, 1966, p. 81.
3. Lincoln. *Red Victory,* p. 85.
4. Quoted in Evan Mawdsley. *The Russian Civil War.* New York: Pegasus Books, 2007, p. 21.
5. Quoted in Samuel Hendel. *The Soviet Crucible: The Soviet System in Theory and Practice.* 4th ed. Belmont CA: Wadsworth, 1973, p. 97.
6. Mawdsley. *The Russian Civil War,* p. 52.
7. Stephen M. Walt. *Revolution and War.* Ithaca NY: Cornell University Press, 1996, pp. 154–155.
8. Quoted in Clifford Kinvig. *Churchill's Crusade: The British Invasion of Russia, 1918–1920.* London: Hambledon Continuum, 2006, p. 292.
9. *New York Times.* "Bolshevism Is Spreading," November 24, 1918, p. 3. http://query.nytimes.com/mem/archive-free/pdf?res=9406E1DA1239E13ABC4C51DFB7678383609EDE.
10. *New York Times.* "Seattle Cars Run; Strike Near End," February 10, 1919, p. 1. http://query.nytimes.com/mem/archive-free/pdf?res=9807EEDE1139E13ABC4852DFB4668382609EDE.
11. *Bolshevik Propaganda: Hearings Before a Subcommittee of the Committee on the Judiciary, and Thereafter, Pursuant to S. Res. 439 and 469. 65th Cong.* February 11, 1919, to March 10, 1919, p. 6.
12. *New York Times.* "Francis Confirms All the Horrors of Bolshevism," March 9, 1919, p. 1. http://query.nytimes.com/mem/archive-free/pdf?res=9E01EEDE1E39E13ABC4153DFB5668382609EDE.
13. *New York Times.* "Tells Senators of Mass Terror by Bolsheviki," February 12, 1919, p. 1. http://query.nytimes.com/mem/archive-free/pdf?res=9803E0DD1139E13ABC4A52DFB4668382609EDE.
14. *New York Times.* "Says the Riffraff, Not the Toilers, Rule in Russia," February 17, 1919, p. 1. http://query.nytimes.com/mem/archive-free/pdf?res=9900EFDB1139E13ABC4F52DFB4668382609EDE.
15. Robert K. Murray. *Red Scare: A Study in National Hysteria, 1919–1920.* St. Paul: University of Minnesota Press, 1955, p. 95.

16. Ann Hagedorn. *Savage Peace: Hope and Fear in America, 1919.* New York: Simon & Schuster, 2007, pp. 421–422.

17. Quoted in Bud Schultz and Ruth Schultz. *It Did Happen Here: Political Repression in America.* Berkeley and Los Angeles: University of California Press, 1989, p. 162.

18. Hagedorn, *Savage Peace*, p. 422.

19. Ellen Schrecker. *Many Are the Crimes: McCarthyism in America.* Boston: Little, Brown, 1998, p. 13.

20. Georgia General Assembly. "Teacher's Oath of Allegiance, No.54: A Resolution," March 26, 1935. http://georgiainfo.galileo.usg.edu/1935resn-3.htm.

21. Ellen Schrecker, "Anti-Communism in America: The World of the Witch Hunters." In *American Inquisition: The Era of McCarthyism* (sound recording). Prince Frederick, MD: Modern Scholar/Recorded Books, 2004, Lecture 3.

22. Ellen Schrecker, "Communism in America: The World of the Witches." In *American Inquisition: The Era of McCarthyism* (sound recording). Prince Frederick, MD: Modern Scholar/Recorded Books, 2004, Lecture 2.

23. Schrecker, *Many Are the Crimes*, p. 17.

Chapter Two: "Our Job ... Shall Be to Rout Them Out"

24. Winston Churchill. "The Sinews of Peace," March 5, 1946. www.winstonchurchill.org/component/content/article/3-speeches/120-the-sinews-of-peace.

25. Harry S. Truman. "The President's News Conference of June 29, 1950," Teaching American History. http://teachingamericanhistory.org/library/index.asp?document=594.

26. Quoted in *New York Times*. "'Foreignism' Fight by Elks Pledged," July 9, 1946, n.p. http://query.nytimes.com/mem/archive/pdf?res=F60811FB3E5C107A93CBA9178CD85F428485F9.

27. Quoted in C.P. Trussell. "Marcantonio and De Lacy Listed by American Action for Defeat." *New York Times*, October 16, 1946, p. 30. http://query.nytimes.com/mem/archive/pdf?res=F70B10F8395C14738DDDAF0994D8415B8688F1D3.

28. Quoted in *New York Times*. "Taft Asks We Stop Appeasing Russia," September 12, 1946, n.p. http://query.nytimes.com/mem/archive/pdf?res=F10E12FE3D5C127A93C0A81782D85F428485F9.

29. Quoted in *New York Times*. "Marcantonio Race Divides a Family," October 23, 1946, n.p. http://query.nytimes.com/mem/archive/pdf?res=FB0712FF3B5C107A93C1AB178BD95F428485F9.

30. Quoted in *New York Times*. "To Keep Up Inquiry in Spite of 'Purge,'" November 27, 1946, p. 4. http://query.nytimes.com/mem/archive/pdf?res=F60B11F93F5B127A93C5AB178AD95F428485F9.

31. David McCullough. *Truman.* New York: Simon & Schuster, 1992, p. 550.

32. Quoted in McCullough. *Truman*, pp. 550–551.

33. Quoted in Robert Justin Goldstein, "Prelude to McCarthyism: The

Making of a Blacklist," *Prologue*, Fall 2006. www.archives.gov/pub lications/prologue/2006/fall/ agloso.html.

34. Quoted in *Time*. "The First Loyalty." National Affairs, March 31, 1947. www.time.com/time/magazine/ article/0,9171,793465,00. html#ixzz1KdkfXIhL.

35. Executive Order 9835, March 21, 1947. www.trumanlibrary.org/ex ecutiveorders/index.php?pid= 502&st=9835&st1=.

36. Quoted in *New York Times*. "President's Order on Loyalty Hailed," March 23, 1947, n.p. http://query. nytimes.com/mem/archive/pdf?r es=F70A16FC3F5A147B93C1AB178 8D85F438485F9.

37. Quoted in *New York Times*. "President's Order on Loyalty Hailed."

38. Quoted in *New York Times*. "President's Order on Loyalty Hailed."

39. Quoted in McCullough. *Truman*, p. 552.

40. Quoted in McCullough. *Truman*, p. 367.

41. McCullough. *Truman*, p. 367.

42. Quoted in McCullough. *Truman*, p. 367.

43. Quoted in McCullough. *Truman*, p. 550.

44. Quoted in McCullough. *Truman*, p. 553.

45. Quoted in William A. Klingaman. *Encyclopedia of the McCarthy Era*. New York: Facts On File, 1996, p. 418.

46. Quoted in Ellen Schrecker. *The Age of McCarthyism: A Brief History with Documents*. 2nd ed. New York: Bedford/St. Martin's, 2002, p. 117.

47. Schrecker. *The Age of McCarthyism*, p. 113.

48. Quoted in Goldstein. "Prelude to McCarthyism."

Chapter Three: "My Loyalty Was Constantly Questioned"

49. *Counterattack*, December 19, 1947, p. 2. www.bloomu.edu/library/ Archives/SC/RadicalNewsletters/ Counterattack/19471219.pdf.

50. Harry S. Truman. "Veto of the Taft-Hartley Labor Bill," June 20, 1947. www.presidency.ucsb.edu/ws/in dex.php?pid=12675#axzz1Uftw F8lQ.

51. *New York Times*. "Workers Must Take Loyalty Oath or Quit," July 21, 1948, p. 2. http://query.nytimes. com/mem/archive/pdf?res=F30E 14FD385C147A93C3AB178CD85F 4C8485F9.

52. Quoted in Schultz and Schultz. *It Did Happen Here*, p. 390.

53. Schrecker. *Many Are the Crimes*, p. 133.

54. Quoted in Benjamin Pine. "Educators Insist on Ouster of Reds." *New York Times*, May 30, 1949, p. 14. http://query.nytimes.com/mem/ archive/pdf?res=F10610F83B58177 B93C2AA178ED85F4D8485F9.

55. Quoted in Pine. "Educators Insist on Ouster of Reds."

56. Quoted in *New York Times*. "Faculty Anti-Red Oaths Set by University of California," June 13, 1949, p. 1. http://query.nytimes.com/mem/ archive/pdf?res=F60917FD395B16 7B93C1A8178DD85F4D8485F9.

57. *New York Times*. "Faculty Anti-Red Oaths Set by University of California."

58. *New York Times*. "California Revises Its 'Loyalty Oath,'" June 25, 1949,

p. 2. http://query.nytimes.com/mem/archive/pdf?res=F20612FD3A5A157B93C7AB178DD85F4D8485F9.

59. Quoted in *New York Times*. "California Court Hears Oath Fight," December 23, 1950, n.p. http://query.nytimes.com/mem/archive/pdf?res=FA0814F9355D147B93C1AB1789D95F448585F9.

60. Quoted in *New York Times*. "California Court Hears Oath Fight."

61. Quoted in Lawrence C. Davis. "U. of California Loyalty Oath Voided by State's High Court," *New York Times*, October 18, 1952, p. 1. http://query.nytimes.com/mem/archive/pdf?res=F70611FD3C5D157B93CAA8178BD95F468585F9.

62. Schrecker. *Many Are the Crimes*, p. 283.

63. Quoted in Schrecker. *Many Are the Crimes*, p. 267.

64. Schultz and Schultz. *It Did Happen Here*, pp. 180–181.

65. Quoted in Schultz and Schultz. *It Did Happen Here*, pp. 179–180.

66. Schultz and Schultz. *It Did Happen Here*, p. 378.

67. Schultz and Schultz. *It Did Happen Here*, p. 377.

68. Schrecker. "Anti-Communism in America."

Chapter Four: "Are You Now, or Have You Ever Been ..."

69. Quoted in C.P. Trussell. "Red 'Underground' in Federal Posts Alleged by Editor," *New York Times*, August 3, 1948, p. 1. http://query.nytimes.com/mem/archive/pdf?res=F60C1FF8345A107A93C6A91783D85F4C8485F9.

70. C.P. Trussell. "President Is Blunt," *New York Times*, August 6, 1948, p. 1. http://query.nytimes.com/mem/archive/pdf?res=F30A11FF3F5C1B7B93C4A91783D85F4C8485F9.

71. Quoted in *New York Times*. "Two Hiss Brothers Deny Red Charges," August 4, 1948, n.p. http://query.nytimes.com/mem/archive/pdf?res=FA0A1FF8345A107A93C6A91783D85F4C8485F9.

72. *Hearings Regarding Communist Espionage in the United States Government, United States House of Representatives, Special Subcommittee of the Committee on Un-American Activities*, August 17, 1948, statement of Whittaker Chambers. http://law2.umkc.edu/faculty/projects/ftrials/hiss/8-17testimony.html.

73. Quoted in Samuel A. Tower. "Film Men Admit Activity by Reds; Hold It Is Foiled," *New York Times*, October 21, 1947, p. 1. http://query.nytimes.com/mem/archive/pdf?res=F30F12FF385E17738DDDA80A94D8415B8788F1D3.

74. Quoted in Albert Fried. *McCarthyism: The Great American Red Scare—a Document History*. New York: Oxford University Press, 1997, p. 41.

75. Quoted in Joseph A. Loftus. "3 More Film Writers Face House Contempt Citations," *New York Times*, October 29, 1947, p. 1. http://query.nytimes.com/mem/archive/pdf?res=F10E17F9385E17738DDDA00A94D8415B8788F1D3.

76. Quoted in Schultz and Schultz. *It Did Happen Here*, p. 131.

77. Quoted in Schultz and Schultz. *It Did Happen Here*, p. 134.

78. Quoted in Schrecker. *The Age of McCarthyism*, p. 59.

79. Quoted in David M. Oshinsky. *A Conspiracy So Immense: The World of Joe McCarthy.* New York: Free Press, 1983, p. 109.

80. Quoted in Oshinsky. *A Conspiracy So Immense,* p. 110.

81. Haynes Johnson. *The Age of Anxiety: McCarthyism to Terrorism.* Orlando, FL: Harcourt, 2005, p. 20.

82. Quoted in Oshinsky. *A Conspiracy So Immense,* p. 118.

83. Quoted in Klingaman. *Encyclopedia of the McCarthy Era,* p. 372.

84. Quoted in Johnson. *The Age of Anxiety,* p. 191.

85. Quoted in William S. White. "Senators Get Lattimore Note Backing Russian Policy in '38." *New York Times,* July 26, 1951, p. 1. http://query.nytimes.com/mem/archive/pdf?res=F60910FA38591A7B93C4AB178CD85F458585F9.

86. Johnson. *The Age of Anxiety,* p. 258.

87. Quoted in Johnson. *The Age of Anxiety,* p. 266.

88. Quoted in Klingaman. *Encyclopedia of the McCarthy Era,* p. 25.

89. Quoted in Klingaman. *Encyclopedia of the McCarthy Era,* p. 25.

90. Quoted in Klingaman. *Encyclopedia of the McCarthy Era,* p. 143.

Chapter Five: Downfall and Aftermath

91. "The Case of Milo Radulovich, A0539839," *See It Now* (TV program), October 20, 1953.

92. "The Case of Milo Radulovich, A0539839."

93. "The Case of Milo Radulovich, A0539839."

94. Thomas Rosteck. *"See It Now" Confronts McCarthyism.* Tuscaloosa: University of Alabama Press, 1994, p. 76.

95. "A Report on Senator Joseph R. McCarthy," *See It Now* (TV program), March 9, 1954.

96. "A Report on Senator Joseph R. McCarthy."

97. Quoted in *Time.* "The Self-Inflated Target." National Affairs, March 22, 1954. www.time.com/time/magazine/article/0,9171,819554-5,00.html.

98. Johnson. *The Age of Anxiety,* p. 391.

99. Quoted in Oshinsky. *A Conspiracy So Immense,* p. 460.

100. Quoted in Johnson, *The Age of Anxiety,* p. 424.

101. *Special Senate Investigation on Charges and Countercharges Involving Secretary of the Army Robert T. Stevens, John G. Adams, H. Struve Hensel, and Senator Joe McCarthy, Roy M. Cohn, and Francis P. Carr Before the Senate Permanent Subcommittee on Investigations of the Committee on Government Operations,* 83rd Cong., June 9, 1954, statement of Joseph Nye Welch. www.youtube.com/watch?v=PTwDUpbQHJg.

102. Quoted in Oshinsky. *A Conspiracy So Immense,* p. 464.

103. Quoted in Klingaman. *Encyclopedia of the McCarthy Era,* p. 145.

104. Harry Johnston. "'Just A Moment, Senator.'" *Life,* October 4, 1954, p. 41. http://books.google.com/books?id=X1IEAAAAMBAJ&pg=PA41&dq#v=onepage&q&f=false.

105. United States Supreme Court. *Mesarosh v. United States,* 352 U.S. 1 (1956), November 5, 1956. http://supreme.justia.com/us/352/1/case.html.

106. United States Supreme Court. *Sweezy v. New Hampshire*, 354 U.S. 234 (1957), June 17, 1957. Available at http://supreme.justia.com/us/354/234/case.html.

107. *Life.* "A Fiery Career's Quiet Close," May 13, 1957, p. 38. http://books.google.com/books?id=Jj8EAAAAMBAJ&pg=PA38&dq#v=onepage&q&f=false.

108. Schrecker. *Many Are the Crimes*, p. 305.

109. Schrecker. *The Age of McCarthyism*, p. 92.

For More Information

Books

Philip S. Foner. *History of the Labor Movement in the United States: Post-War Struggles, 1918–1920.* New York: International, 1988. Foner presents concise summaries of many of the important strikes during the first Red Scare, along with histories of the Socialist and Communist Parties and the Palmer Raids.

Albert Fried. *McCarthyism: The Great American Red Scare—a Document History.* New York: Oxford University Press, 1997. This anthology has a wide variety of original source documents, from loyalty-security board hearings to congressional testimonies.

Haynes Johnson. *The Age of Anxiety: McCarthyism to Terrorism.* Orlando, FL: James H. Silberman/Harcourt, 2005. Journalist Haynes Johnson presents a fascinating look at the McCarthy period, with a special emphasis on media coverage, in the first half of the book and then draws parallels to the current world events surrounding post-9/11 terrorism.

William K. Klingaman. *Encyclopedia of the McCarthy Era.* New York: Facts On File, 1996. This book presents a wide range of biographical and topical information about the period. Some entries are more extensive than others, and some noteworthy individuals (such as Milo Radulovich) are mentioned only in other entries.

David M. Oshinsky. *A Conspiracy So Immense: The World of Joe McCarthy.* New York: Free Press, 1983. This work documents the rise and fall of McCarthy, with a number of highly illustrative anecdotes about the senator's life, including excellent information about his last years of life.

Ellen Schrecker. *The Age of McCarthyism: A Brief History with Documents.* New York: St. Martin's, 1994. This volume presents short topical summaries of the period's main topics to introduce historical documents that highlight the era, such as one version of McCarthy's Wheeling speech and the roster of individuals found in *Red Channels*.

Ellen Schrecker. *Many Are the Crimes: McCarthyism in America.* Boston: Little, Brown, 1998. In this work, Schrecker presents an overall study of the era, with particular emphasis on the individuals who helped create the anti-Red fervor and those who were affected by it.

Bud Schultz and Ruth Schultz. *It Did Happen Here: Political Repression in America.* Berkeley and Los Angeles: University of California Press, 1989. Oral historians Bud and Ruth Schultz interview a cross-section of

Americans caught up in political repression, including many who were involved in the Red Scare.

Periodicals and Internet Sources

Life. "A Fiery Career's Quiet Close," May 13, 1957.

Life. "'Just A Moment, Senator,'" October 4, 1954.

New York Times. "Faculty Anti-Red Oaths Set by University of California," June 13, 1949.

New York Times. "Francis Confirms All the Horrors of Bolshevism," March 9, 1919.

New York Times. "President's Order on Loyalty Hailed," March 23, 1947.

New York Times. "Red 'Underground' in Federal Posts Alleged by Editor," August 3, 1948.

New York Times. "3 More Film Writers Face House Contempt Citations," October 29, 1947.

New York Times. "To Keep Up Inquiry in Spite of 'Purge,'" November 27, 1946.

New York Times. "Workers Must Take Loyalty Oath or Quit," July 21, 1948.

Margaret Chase Smith. "A Declaration of Conscience." www.senate.gov/ artandhistory/history/resources/ pdf/SmithDeclaration.pdf.

Time. "The First Loyalty." National Affairs, March 31, 1947.

Time. "The Self-Inflated Target." National Affairs, March 22, 1954.

Audio/Video

The Edward R. Murrow Television Collection. Four-disc set (CBS Inc./Docurama, 2005). Contains a retrospective of the pioneering journalist. Volume 3, "The McCarthy Years," contains the full broadcasts of the four *See It Now* programs related to McCarthyism, including "The Case of Milo Radulovich, A0589839."

Good Night, and Good Luck. Directed by George Clooney. Warner Independent Pictures, 2005. A dramatized re-creation of the events at CBS related to the McCarthy *See It Now* broadcasts in 1953 and 1954. Using archival footage of contemporary figures, the film re-creates the decisions undertaken by Edward R. Murrow and Fred Friendly as they took on Senator McCarthy.

Ellen Schrecker. *American Inquisition: The Era of McCarthyism.* Prince Frederick, MD: Modern Scholar/ Recorded Books, 2004, audio book, 7 compact discs, 8 hrs. Schrecker reads lectures based on several of her works on McCarthyism and the Red Scare.

Websites

The Alger Hiss Trials (http://law2. umkc.edu/faculty/projects/ftri als/hiss/hiss.html). The University of Missouri–Kansas City Law School's Famous Trials site includes a chronology of the events, transcripts of testimonies and court cases, and video clips.

Counterattack (www.bloomu.edu/libr ary/Archives/SC/RadicalNewslet ters/Counterattack/counterattack. htm). A Bloomsburg University website dedicated to radical newsletters of the past, including the Red Scare era *Counterattack*. Each digitized edition is summarized on the main page, followed by a link to the PDF version of the newsletter.

Edward R. Murrow, See It Now, March 9, 1954 (http://www.youtube.com/watch?v=anNEJJYLU8M&feature=grec_index). Murrow's closing commentary from the *See It Now* episode about McCarthy.

Life **Magazine Archive** (http://books.google.com/books/about/LIFE.html?id=R1cEAAAAMBAJ). *Life* magazine was a popular weekly newsmagazine that helped Americans learn about their nation and the world from the 1930s through the 1970s. It was famous for its stunning black-and-white photos. Senator McCarthy, the Korean War, and Communists around the world were featured prominently during the second Red Scare period. The magazine's archives are available through Google Books (http://books.google.com). The archive has a customizable index that allows readers to search by topic and by date range.

The New York Times Archive (http://query.nytimes.com/search/sitesearch). The archive contains digitized copies of its newspapers from 1851 to the present. It has a customizable index that allows readers to search by topic and by date range. Articles from certain dates are free to access; others can be purchased singly or by subscription, with educational discounts available.

Seattle General Strike Project (http://depts.washington.edu/labhist/strike/). The University of Washington's site has a treasure trove of information related to the Seattle General Strike of 1919, including links to oral histories and a database of almost two hundred digitized news articles from the time.

Welch vs. Joseph McCarthy (www.youtube.com/watch?v=Po5GlFba5Yg and www.youtube.com/watch? v=PTwDUpbQHJg). The interplay between McCarthy and army counsel Frank Welch is provided in two parts.

The Winston Churchill Centre and Museum (www.winstonchurchill.org/learn/speeches/speeches-of-winston-churchill/120-the-sinews-of-peace). Full text of Winston Churchill's "The Sinews of Peace" speech March 5, 1946 (better known as the "Iron Curtain" speech) and video of the "Iron Curtain" portion of the speech are available at this website.

Index

Treaty of Brest-Litovsk, 17
Truman, Harry S., *33* , *40*
  on Communism, 37
  Executive Order 9835, 38–39
  on FBI investigation practices,
    40, 41
  on Federal Employee Loyalty
    Program, 40
  foreign policy, 29–30, 32, 33
  Hoover relationship, 41
  national security addition to
    loyalty act, 54
  Taft-Hartley Act veto, 49
Trumbo, Dalton, 67, 90
Tydings, Millard, 74

U
Ulyanov,Vladimir I. *See* Lenin
United Nations, 32
United States, Mesarosh v. (1956), 87
University of California, 52–54
U.S. Army investigations by
  McCarthy Senate Committee, 75–76
U.S. Coast Guard loyalty-security
  regulations, 55–57
U.S. Postal Service loyalty-security
  regulations, 55–57
U.S. Senate, 74–78

V
Vanech, A. Devitt, 37
Victims, 89–90

W
Walt, Stephen, M., 17
Warren, Earl, 53, 87
Watkins, Arthur, 86–87
Watkins Committee, 86–87
Weigel, Stanley, 54
Welch, Joseph Nye, 84–86, *85*
Wershba, Joseph, 80, 91, 92
Whitney, Samuel G., 49
Wilson, Woodrow, 17
Wiretapping, 59
Wood, Sam, 66–67
Workplace fear and insecurity, 49,
  50–51, 55, 56, 57
World events, 64–65, 70, 74
World War II, 29–30

Y
Yarmolinsky, Adam, 55
Young, Cole v. (1956), 87–88, 90

Z
Zwicker, Ralph, 75–76, *76*, 82, 83

Picture Credits

Cover: © Bettmann/Corbis
© Bettmann/Corbis, 6, 43, 50, 62, 65, 68, 73, 87
© Classic Image/Alamy, 11
© David Cole/Alamy, 6
© Everett Collection Inc/Alamy, 36, 52, 67
© H. Armstrong Roberts/ClassicStock/Corbis, 55
Alfred Eisenstaedt/Pix Inc./Time Life Pictures/Getty Images, 27
Alfred Eisenstaedt/Time & Life Pictures/Getty Images, 82
Allan Grant/Time Life Pictures/Getty Images, 7
AP Images, 40, 85, 89
AP Images/Alik Keplicz, 91
AP Images/Byron Rollins, 33
AP Images/Detroit Free Press, 80
AP Images/Dwayne Newton, 71

AP Images/Jacob Harris, 58
AP Images/NY Times, 6
Archive Photos/Getty Images, 24
Fox Photos/Getty Images, 31
George Skadding/Time Life Pictures/Getty Images, 46, 60
Grey Villet/Time Life Pictures/Getty Images, 84
Hank Walker/Time Life Pictures/Getty Images, 76
Hulton Archive/Getty Images, 16, 42
Keystone/Getty Images, 7, 14
PhotoQuest/Getty Images, 20
Tony Linck/Time & Life Pictures/Getty Images, 48
Universal History Archive/Getty Images, 18
Walter Sanders/Time Life Pictures/Getty Images, 30

About the Author

Andrew A. Kling worked as a National Park Service ranger across the United States for over fifteen years. He now works as a writer and editor for a variety of nonprofit organizations and as an interpretive media developer and consultant. He enjoys hockey and history, technology and trivia, books, movies, flags, and spending time with his wife and their famous Norwegian Forest cat, Chester.